Documenting Sources Across the Curriculum

Documenting Sources Across the Curriculum

adapted from

The Little, Brown Handbook

Eighth Edition

Longman

New York San Francisco Boston
London Toronto Sydney Tokyo Singapore Madrid
Mexico City Munich Paris Cape Town Hong Kong Montreal

Documenting Sources Across the Curriculum, Eighth Edition

Please visit our Web site at *http://www.awlonline.com/littlebrown*.

ISBN 0-321-07761-X

1 2 3 4 5 6 7 8 9 10—CRW—03 02 01 00

Contents

Preface

Documenting Sources across the Curriculum, adapted from *The Little, Brown Handbook,* Eighth Edition, is designed to be a fast, easy reference for students writing research papers in the humanities, social sciences, and natural sciences. All of the information in this guide is derived from Part X, "Researching Writing," and Part XI, "Writing in the Academic Disciplines," in *The Little, Brown Handbook,* Eighth Edition.

The handy research paper schedule (following this preface) will help you manage your research project.

Chapter 1, "Making a Working Bibliography," lists what publication information to document in your working bibliography while you are gathering your sources.

The last four chapters cover four common styles:

- The formats of the Modern Language Association (MLA), used in English, foreign languages, and some other humanities (Chapter 2).
- The formats of the *Chicago Manual of Style* (CMS), often used in history, art, and some other humanities (Chapter 3).
- The formats of the American Psychological Association (APA), widely used in the social sciences (Chapter 4).
- The formats of the Council of Biology Editors (CBE), widely used in the sciences (Chapter 5).
- The formats of the Columbia style for online sources in the humanities and the social and natural sciences (Chapter 6).

For more specific information, consult *The Little, Brown Handbook* or *The Little, Brown Compact Handbook.*

Scheduling steps in research writing

Complete by:

1. Setting a schedule and beginning a research journal
2. Finding a researchable topic and question
3. Developing a research strategy
4. Finding sources, both print and electronic, and making a working bibliography

---

5. Evaluating and synthesizing sources
6. Taking notes using summary, paraphrase, and direct quotation and avoiding plagiarism
7. Developing a thesis statement

---

8. Creating a structure
9. Drafting the paper, integrating summaries, paraphrases, and direct quotations into your ideas

---

10. Revising and editing the paper
11. Citing sources in your text
12. Preparing the list of works cited
13. Preparing and proofreading the final manuscript

Final paper due

Each segment marked off by a horizontal line will occupy *roughly* one-fourth of the total time. The most unpredictable segments are the first two, so it's wise to get started early enough to accommodate the unexpected.

Documenting Sources Across the Curriculum

CHAPTER 1

Making a Working Bibliography

When you begin searching for sources, it may be tempting to pursue each possibility as you come across it. But that approach would prove inefficient and probably ineffective. Instead, you'll want to find out the full range of sources available and then decide on a good number to consult. For a paper of 1800 to 2500 words, try for ten to thirty promising titles as a start.

To keep track of where sources are and what they are, make a **working bibliography**, a file of books, articles, Web sites, and other possibilities. When you have a substantial file, you can decide which sources seem most promising and look them up first or, if necessary, order them through interlibrary loan.

A working bibliography is your chance to record all the information you need to find your sources and, eventually, to acknowledge them in your paper.

1a Tracking source information

You have several options for making a working bibliography:

- Copy source information by hand on note cards (usually 3″ × 5″), one source to a card. With this system, you can record source information no matter where you are, as long as you have a pen or pencil, and you can easily add, delete, and rearrange sources. Some instructors require that a working bibliography be submitted on note cards.
- Keep the working bibliography on your computer's hard drive or a diskette. You'll be able to sort sources by topic or by author and to copy bibliographic data into your paper when you prepare final source citations.
- Combine the previous two systems: print and cut up computer-generated source listings, and then paste or tape each source on a note card.

1b Recording source information

When you turn in your paper, you will be expected to attach a list of the sources you have used. So that readers can check or follow up on your sources, your list must include all the information needed to find the sources, in a format readers can understand. The box below shows the information you should record for each type of source so that you will not have to retrace your steps later.

Most academic disciplines require special formats for source citations, and several are presented in this book:

- Modern Language Association (MLA) style, used in English, foreign languages, and some other humanities (pp. 5–36).

Information for a working bibliography

For books

Library call number
Name(s) of author(s), editor(s), translator(s), or others listed
Title and subtitle
Publication data:
  Place of publication
  Publisher's name
  Date of publication
Other important data, such as edition or volume number

For periodical articles

Name(s) of author(s)
Title and subtitle of article
Title of periodical
Publication data:
  Volume number and issue number (if any) in which article appears
  Date of issue
  Page numbers on which article appears

For electronic sources

Name(s) of author(s)
Title and subtitle
Publication data if source is also published in print
Electronic publication data:
  Date of release, online posting, or latest revision
  Name and vendor (or publisher) of a database or name of an online service or network (America Online, Lexis-Nexis, etc.)
  Medium (CD-ROM, online, etc.)
  Format of online source (Web page, e-mail, etc.)
Date you consulted the source
Search terms used to reach the source (for a database)
Complete electronic address

For other sources

Name(s) of author(s) or others listed, such as a government department or a recording artist
Title of the work
Format, such as unpublished letter or live performance
Publication or production data:
  Publisher's or producer's name
  Date of publication, release, or production
  Identifying numbers (if any)

- Chicago style, used in history, art history, religion, philosophy, and some other humanities (pp. 37–45).
- American Psychological Association (APA) style, used in psychology and other social sciences (pp. 46–60).
- Council of Biology Editors (CBE) style, used in the biological and other sciences (pp. 61–68).
- Columbia style for online sources in the humanities and the social and natural sciences (pp. 69–79).

Before compiling your working bibliography, ask your instructor what documentation style you should use. Then consult the relevant handbook section to determine what kind of information to include and how to arrange it.

Note Computerized bibliography programs can help you format your source citations in an appropriate academic style.

1c Finding bibliographic information for online sources

Unlike that for printed materials, publication information for online sources can be difficult to find and make sense of. The screen shot opposite shows the first page of a Web site. Circled numbers refer to the numbered explanations following.

1. The source's address, or URL, usually appears in the Web browser's Address or Location field near the top of the screen. If the field does not appear, adjust the settings of the browser so that it displays the field.
2. Use as the source title the title of the page you are consulting. This information usually appears as a heading at the top of the page, but if not it may also appear in the bar along the top of the browser window. When the page heading and the browser title differ, generally choose the browser title because it is the information used for bookmarks and search engines. However, if the browser title conveys no information—for instance, *Home Page*—then use the page heading.
3. Important information often appears at or near the bottom of each page. Look here for (*a*) the name of the author or the sponsoring organization, (*b*) an address for reaching the sponsor or author directly, and (*c*) the publication date or the date of the last revision.

If the page you are reading does not list publication information, look for it on the site's home page. There may be a link to the home page, or you can find it by editing the address in the Address or Location field: working backward, delete the end of the address

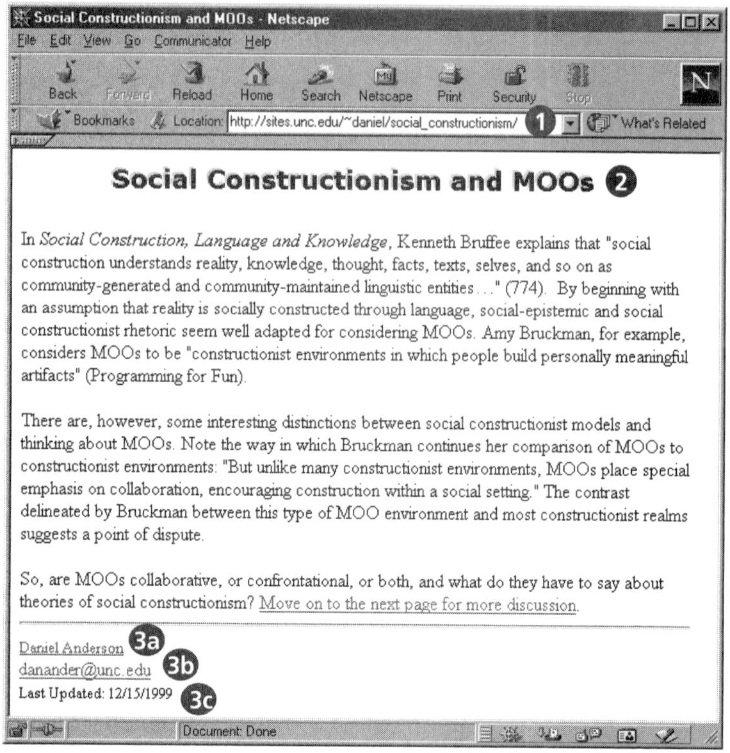

up to the preceding slash; then hit Enter. (For the address in the screen shot, you would delete *social_constructionism/*.) If that action doesn't take you to the home page, delete the end of the remaining address up to the preceding slash and hit Enter. Editing the address in this way, you'll eventually reach the home page.

When scouting a discussion list, Web forum, or newsgroup, save messages that may serve as sources, and keep track of when and where they were posted. You may be able to discover information about the author of a message from the list's archive or from an archive site such as Deja (*http://www.deja.com*).

CHAPTER 2

MLA Style

2a Understanding MLA style

The documentation system of the Modern Language Association is detailed in the *MLA Handbook for Writers of Research Papers,* 5th edition (1999). This style employs brief parenthetical citations within the text that direct readers to the list of works cited. For example:

Only one article mentions this discrepancy (Wolfe 62).

The name Wolfe directs readers to the article by Wolfe in the list of works cited, and the page number 62 specifies the page in the article on which the cited material appears.

The following pages describe this documentation system: what must be included in a citation (below), where to place citations (p. 11), when to use footnotes or endnotes in addition to parenthetical citations (p. 12), and how to create the list of works cited (p. 13). The index on the next page (parenthetical text citations) and the one on pages 14–15 (works-cited entries) provide quick-reference guides to the models.

2b Citing sources in your text: MLA style

1 Writing parenthetical text citations

In-text citations of sources have two requirements:

- They must include just enough information for the reader to locate the appropriate source in your list of works cited.
- They must include just enough information for the reader to locate the place in the source where the material appears.

http://www.mla.org/main_stl.htm The MLA Web site, offering occasional updates of MLA style and answers to frequently asked questions.

http://owl.english.purdue.edu/Files/34.html Guidance on using MLA style, from the Purdue Online Writing Lab.

MLA parenthetical text citations

Usually, you can meet both these requirements by providing the author's last name and the page(s) in the source on which the material appears. The reader can find the source in your list of works cited and find the borrowed material in the source itself.

Note For most sources, you will provide the author's or authors' last names and a page reference. Do not include the title unless you are citing more than one work by exactly the same author(s) or the source has no listed author (models 8 and 9, pp. 8–9). The following examples cite a book to which neither of these exceptions applies.

Not One text discusses the "ethical dilemmas in public relations practice" (Wilcox, Ault, and Agee, Public Relations 125).

Not One text discusses the "ethical dilemmas in public relations practice" (Public Relations 125).

But One text discusses the "ethical dilemmas in public relations practice" (Wilcox, Ault, and Agee 125).

1. Author not named in your text

When you have not already named the author in your sentence, provide the author's last name and the page number(s), with no punctuation between them, in parentheses.

> One researcher concludes that "women impose a distinctive construction on moral problems, seeing moral dilemmas in terms of conflicting responsibilities" (Gilligan 105).

See models 5 and 6 (pp. 7–8) for the forms to use when the source does not provide page numbers.

2. Author named in your text

If the author's name is already given in your text, you need not repeat it in the parenthetical citation. The citation gives just the page number(s).

> One researcher, Carol Gilligan, concludes that "women impose a distinctive construction on moral problems, seeing moral dilemmas in terms of conflicting responsibilities" (105).

3. A work with two or three authors

If the source has two or three authors, give all their last names in the text or in the citation. Separate two authors' names with "and":

> As Frieden and Sagalyn observe, "The poor and the minorities were the leading victims of highway and renewal programs" (29).

> According to one study, "The poor and the minorities were the leading victims of highway and renewal programs" (Frieden and Sagalyn 29).

With three authors, add commas and also "and" before the final name:

> The text by Wilcox, Ault, and Agee discusses the "ethical dilemmas in public relations practice" (125).

> One text discusses the "ethical dilemmas in public relations practice" (Wilcox, Ault, and Agee 125).

4. A work with more than three authors

If the source has more than three authors, you may list all their last names or use only the first author's name followed by "et al." (the abbreviation for the Latin *et alii,* "and others"). The choice depends on what you do in your list of works cited (see p. 16).

> It took the combined forces of the Americans, Europeans, and Japanese to break the rebel siege of Beijing in 1900 (Lopez et al. 362).

> It took the combined forces of the Americans, Europeans, and Japanese to break the rebel siege of Beijing in 1900 (Lopez, Blum, Cameron, and Barnes 362).

5. A work with numbered paragraphs or screens instead of pages

Some electronic sources number each paragraph or screen instead of each page. In citing passages in these sources, give the paragraph or screen number(s) and distinguish them from page numbers: after the author's name, put a comma, a space, and "par." (one paragraph), "pars." (more than one paragraph), "screen," or "screens."

> Twins reared apart report similar feelings (Palfrey, pars. 6-7).

6. An entire work or a work with no page or other reference numbers

When you cite an entire work rather than a part of it, the citation will not include any page or paragraph number. Try to work the author's name into your text, in which case you will not need a parenthetical citation. But remember that the source must appear in the list of works cited.

> Boyd deals with the need to acknowledge and come to terms with our fear of nuclear technology.

Use the same format when you cite a specific passage from a work with no page or other reference numbers, such as an online source.

If the author's name does not appear in your text, put it in a parenthetical citation.

> Almost 20 percent of commercial banks have been audited for the practice (Friis).

7. A multivolume work

If you consulted only one volume of a multivolume work, your list of works cited will indicate as much (see model 14, pp. 18–19), and you can treat the volume as any book.

If you consulted more than one volume of a multivolume work, give the appropriate volume in your text citation.

> After issuing the Emancipation Proclamation, Lincoln said, "What I did, I did after very full deliberations, and under a very heavy and solemn sense of responsibility" (5: 438).

The number 5 indicates the volume from which the quotation was taken; the number 438 indicates the page number in that volume. When the author's name appears in such a citation, place it before the volume number with no punctuation: (Lincoln 5: 438).

If you are referring generally to an entire volume of a multivolume work and are not citing specific page numbers, add the abbreviation "vol." before the volume number as in (vol. 5) or (Lincoln, vol. 5) (note the comma after the author's name). Then readers will not misinterpret the volume number as a page number.

8. A work by an author of two or more cited works

If your list of works cited includes two or more works by the same author, then your citation must tell the reader which of the author's works you are referring to. Give the title either in the text or in a parenthetical citation. In a parenthetical citation, give the full title only if it is brief; otherwise, shorten the title to the first one or two main words (excluding *A, An,* or *The*).

> At about age seven, children begin to use appropriate gestures with their stories (Gardner, Arts 144-45).

The title *Arts* is shortened from Gardner's full title, *The Arts and Human Development* (see the works-cited entry for this book on p. 16).

9. An unsigned work

Refer to an anonymous source by a full or shortened version of the title, as explained above. In your list of works cited, you will alphabetize an anonymous work by the first main word of the title (see p. 17), so the first word of a shortened title should be the same. This citation refers to an unsigned article titled "The Right to Die."

> One article notes that a death-row inmate may demand his own execution to achieve a fleeting notoriety ("Right").

A page number is unnecessary because the article is no longer than a page (see the entry for the article on p. 23).

10. A government publication or a work with a corporate author

If the author of the work is listed as a government body or a corporation, cite the work by that organization's name. If the name is long, work it into the text to avoid an intrusive parenthetical citation.

> A 1998 report by the Hawaii Department of Education predicts an increase in enrollments (6).

11. An indirect source

When you want to use a quotation that is already in quotation marks—indicating that the author you are reading is quoting someone else—try to find the original source and quote directly from it. If you can't find the original source then your citation must indicate that your quotation of it is indirect. In the following citation, "qtd. in" ("quoted in") says that Davino was quoted by Boyd:

> George Davino maintains that "even small children have vivid ideas about nuclear energy" (qtd. in Boyd 22).

The list of works cited then includes only Boyd (the work consulted), not Davino.

12. A literary work

Novels, plays, and poems are often available in many editions, so your instructor may ask you to provide information that will help readers find the passage you cite no matter what edition they consult.

For novels, the page number comes first, followed by a semicolon and then information on the appropriate part or chapter of the work.

> Toward the end of James's novel, Maggie suddenly feels "the thick breath of the definite--which was the intimate, the immediate, the familiar, as she hadn't had them for so long" (535; pt. 6, ch. 41).

For poems that are not divided into parts, you can omit the page number and supply the line number(s) for the quotation. To prevent confusion with page numbers, precede the numbers with "line" or "lines" in the first citation; then just use the numbers.

> In Shakespeare's Sonnet 73 the speaker identifies with the trees of late autumn, "Bare ruined choirs, where late the sweet birds sang" (line 4). "In me," Shakespeare writes, "thou seest the glowing of such fire / That on the ashes of his youth doth lie" (9-10).

For verse plays and poems that are divided into parts, omit a page number and cite the appropriate part—act (and scene, if any), canto, book, and so on—plus the line number(s). Use Arabic numerals for parts, including acts and scenes (3.4), unless your instructor specifies Roman numerals (III.iv).

> Later in King Lear Shakespeare has the disguised Edgar say, "The prince of darkness is a gentleman" (3.4.147).

For prose plays, provide the page number followed by the act and scene. See the reference to *Death of a Salesman* on page 12.

13. The Bible

When you cite passages of the Bible in parentheses, abbreviate the title of any book longer than four letters—for instance, "Gen." (Genesis), "1 Sam." (1 Samuel), "Ps." (Psalms), "Matt." (Matthew), "Rom." (Romans). Then give the chapter and verse(s) in Arabic numerals.

> According to the Bible, at Babel God "did [. . .] confound the language of all the earth" (Gen. 11.9).

14. An electronic source

Cite an electronic source as you would any other source: usually by author's name or, if there is no author, by title.

> Business forecasts for the fourth quarter tended to be optimistic (White 4).

This source has page numbers. For a source with paragraph or screen numbers or no numbering, see models 5 and 6 (pp. 7–8).

15. More than one work

If you use a parenthetical citation to refer to more than a single work, separate the references with a semicolon.

> Two recent articles point out that a computer badly used can be less efficient than no computer at all (Gough and Hall 201; Richards 162).

Since long citations in the text can distract the reader, you may choose to cite several or more works in an endnote or footnote rather than in the text. See page 12.

2 Positioning and punctuating parenthetical citations

Position text citations to accomplish two goals:

- Make it clear exactly where your borrowing begins and ends.
- Keep the citation as unobtrusive as possible.

You can accomplish both goals by placing the parenthetical citation at the end of the sentence element containing the borrowed material. This sentence element may be a phrase or a clause, and it may begin, interrupt, or conclude the sentence. Usually, as in the examples below, the element ends with a punctuation mark.

> The inflation rate might climb as high as 30 percent (Kim 164), an increase that could threaten the small nation's stability.

> The inflation rate, which might climb as high as 30 percent (Kim 164), could threaten the small nation's stability.

> The small nation's stability could be threatened by its inflation rate, which, one source predicts, might climb as high as 30 percent (Kim 164).

In the last example the addition of *one source predicts* clarifies that Kim is responsible only for the inflation-rate prediction, not for the statement about stability.

For citations in your running text, generally place the parenthetical citation *before* any punctuation required by your sentence, as in the examples above. If the material is a quotation, place the citation *between* the closing quotation mark and the punctuation.

> Spelling argues that during the 1970s American automobile manufacturers met consumer needs "as well as could be expected" (26), but not everyone agrees with him.

The exception is a quotation ending in a question mark or exclamation point. Then use the appropriate punctuation inside the closing quotation mark; follow the quotation with the citation and a period:

> "Of what use is genius," Emerson asks, "if the organ [. . .] cannot find a focal distance within the actual horizon of human life?" ("Experience" 60). Mad genius is no genius.

When a citation appears after a quotation that ends in a bracketed ellipsis mark, place the citation between the closing quotation mark and the sentence period.

> One observer maintains that "American manufacturers must bear the blame for their poor sales [. . .]" (Rosenbaum 12).

When a citation appears at the end of a quotation set off from the text, place it one space *after* the punctuation ending the quotation. No additional punctuation is needed.

> In Arthur Miller's Death of a Salesman, the most poignant defense of Willie Loman comes from his wife, Linda:
>
> > He's not the finest character that ever lived. But he's a human being, and a terrible thing is happening to him. So attention must be paid. He's not to be allowed to fall into his grave like an old dog. Attention, attention must finally be paid to such a person. (56; act 1)

(This citation of a play includes the act number as well as the page number. See p. 10.)

3 Using footnotes or endnotes in special circumstances

Occasionally, you may want to use footnotes or endnotes in place of parenthetical citations. If you need to refer to several sources at once, listing them in a long parenthetical citation could be intrusive. In that case, signal the citation with a numeral raised above the appropriate line of text and write a note with the same numeral to cite the sources:

Text At least five studies have confirmed these results.[1]

Note [1] Abbott and Winger 266-68; Casner 27; Hoyenga 78-79; Marino 36; Tripp, Tripp, and Walk 179-83.

You may also use a footnote or endnote to comment on a source or provide information that does not fit easily in the text:

Text So far, no one has confirmed these results.[2]

Note [2] Manter reports spending a year trying to replicate the experiment, but he was never able to produce the high temperatures reported by the original experimenters (616).

In a note the raised numeral is indented five spaces and followed by a space. If the note appears as a footnote, place it at the bottom of the page on which the citation appears, set it off from the text with quadruple spacing, and single-space the note itself. If the note appears as an endnote, place it in numerical order with the other endnotes on a page between the text and the list of works cited; double-space all the endnotes.

2c Preparing the list of works cited: MLA style

In the documentation style of the *MLA Handbook,* your in-text parenthetical citations (discussed in 2b) refer the reader to complete information on your sources in a list you title "Works Cited" and place at the end of your paper. The list should include all the sources you quoted, paraphrased, or summarized in your paper. (If your instructor asks you to include sources you examined but did not cite, title the list "Works Consulted.")

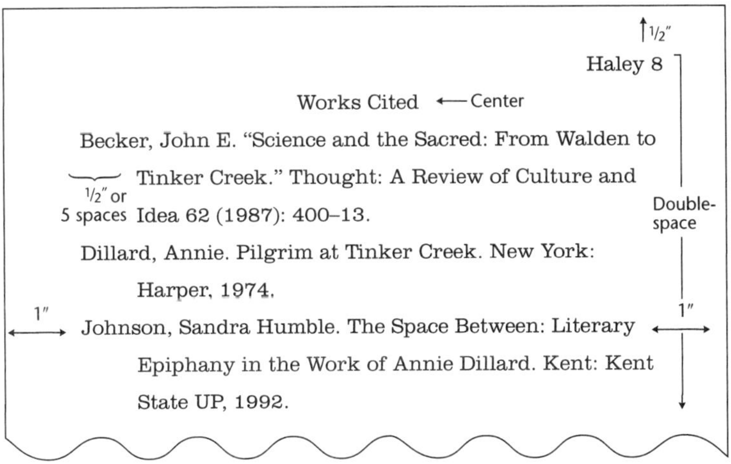

Follow this format for the list of works cited:

- Arrange your sources in alphabetical order by the last name of the author. If an author is not given in the source, alphabetize the source by the first main word of the title (excluding *A, An,* or *The*).
- Type the list double-spaced (within and between entries).
- Indent the second and subsequent lines of each entry one-half inch from the left.

The box on the next page directs you to the MLA formats for works-cited entries. If you can't find a model that exactly matches a source, follow the closest possible match. You can combine formats—for instance, drawing on model 2 and model 26 for a newspaper article with two authors.

MLA works-cited models

1 Listing books

The basic format for a book includes the following elements:

Gilligan, Carol. (①) In a Different Voice: Psychological Theory and Women's Development. (②) Cambridge (ⓐ): Harvard UP (ⓑ), 1982 (ⓒ). (③)

1. *Author.* Use the author's full name: last name first, followed by a comma, and then the first name and any middle name or initial. Omit any title or degree attached to the author's name, such as Dr. or Ph.D. End the name with a period and one space.
2. *Title.* Give the full title, including any subtitle. Underline the title unless your instructor specifically calls for italics. Capitalize all important words, separate the main title and the subtitle with a colon and one space, and end the title with a period and

one space. For citing a part of a book, such as an essay or poem, see model 18 (pp. 19–20).

3. *Publication information.* You can usually find this information on the book's title page or on the copyright page following:

   a. The city of publication, followed by a colon and one space. Use only the first city if the source lists more than one.
   b. The name of the publisher, followed by a comma. Shorten most publishers' names, often to a single word: "Little" for Little, Brown, "Knopf" for Alfred A. Knopf. For university presses, use the abbreviations "U" and "P," as in the example. If the title page lists an imprint and a publisher—for instance, Vintage Books and Random House—give both names with a hyphen: "Vintage-Random."
   c. The date of publication, ending with a period.

When a reference requires other information, generally place it either between the author's name and the title or between the title and the publication information, as specified in the models on the following pages.

1. A book with one author

Gilligan, Carol. In a Different Voice: Psychological Theory and Women's Development. Cambridge: Harvard UP, 1982.

2. A book with two or three authors

Frieden, Bernard J., and Lynne B. Sagalyn. Downtown, Inc.: How America Rebuilds Cities. Cambridge: MIT P, 1989.

Wilcox, Dennis L., Phillip H. Ault, and Warren K. Agee. Public Relations: Strategies and Tactics. 4th ed. New York: Harper, 1999.

Give the authors' names in the order provided on the title page. Reverse the first and last names of the first author *only,* not of any other authors. Separate two authors' names with a comma and "and"; separate three authors' names with commas and with "and" before the third name.

3. A book with more than three authors

Lopez, Robert S., et al. Civilizations: Western and World. Boston: Little, 1975.

You may, but need not, give all authors' names if the work has more than three authors. If you choose not to give all names, provide the name of the first author only, and follow the name with a comma and the abbreviation "et al." (for the Latin *et alii,* meaning "and others").

4. Two or more works by the same author(s)

Gardner, Howard. The Arts and Human Development. New York: Wiley, 1973.

---. The Quest for Mind: Piaget, Lévi-Strauss, and the Structuralist Movement. New York: Knopf, 1973.

Give the author's name only in the first entry. For the second and any subsequent works by the same author, substitute three hyphens for the author's name, followed by a period and one space. Within the set of entries for the author, list the sources alphabetically by the first main word of the title (here "Arts," then "Quest"). Note that the three hyphens stand for *exactly* the same name or names. If the second source above were by Gardner and somebody else, both names would have to be given in full.

5. A book with an editor

Ruitenbeek, Hendrick, ed. Freud as We Knew Him. Detroit: Wayne State UP, 1973.

The abbreviation "ed.," separated from the name by a comma, identifies Ruitenbeek as the editor of the work.

6. A book with an author and an editor

Mumford, Lewis. The City in History. Ed. Donald L. Miller. New York: Pantheon, 1986.

When citing the work of the author, give his or her name first, and give the editor's name after the title, preceded by "Ed." ("Edited by"). When citing the work of the editor, use model 5 for a book with an editor, and give the author's name after the title preceded by "By": Miller, Donald L., ed. The City in History. By Lewis Mumford.

7. A translation

Alighieri, Dante. The Inferno. Trans. John Ciardi. New York: NAL, 1971.

When citing the work of the author, give his or her name first, and give the translator's name after the title, preceded by "Trans." ("Translated by"). When citing the work of the translator, give his or her name first, followed by a comma and "trans."; then follow the title with "By" and the author's name: Ciardi, John, trans. The Inferno. By Dante Alighieri.

When a book you cite by author has a translator *and* an editor, give the translator's and editor's names in the order used on the book's title page. For a translated selection from an edited book, see model 18, pages 19–20.

8. A book with a corporate author

Lorenz Research, Inc. Research in Social Studies Teaching. Baltimore: Arrow, 1997.

List the name of the corporation, institution, or other body as author.

9. An anonymous book

The Dorling Kindersley World Reference Atlas. London: Dorling, 1999.

List an anonymous book by its full title. Alphabetize the book by the title's first main word (here "Dorling"), omitting *A, An,* or *The.*

10. The Bible

The Bible. King James Version.

The New English Bible. London: Oxford UP and Cambridge UP, 1970.

When citing a standard version of the Bible (first example), do not underline the title or the name of the version, and you need not provide publication information. For an edition of the Bible (second example), underline the title and give its full publication information.

11. A later edition

Bollinger, Dwight L. Aspects of Language. 2nd ed. New York: Harcourt, 1975.

For any edition after the first, place the edition number between the title and the publication information. Use the appropriate designation for editions that are named or dated rather than numbered—for instance, "Rev. ed." for "Revised edition."

12. A republished book

James, Henry. The Golden Bowl. 1904. London: Penguin, 1966.

Republished books include paperbound editions of books originally released in hard bindings and books reissued under new titles. Place the original date of publication (but not the place of publication or the publisher's name) after the title, and then provide the full publication information for the source you are using. If the book was originally published under a different title, add this title at the end of the entry and move the original publication date to follow the title—for example, Rpt. of Thomas Hardy: A Life. 1941.

13. A book with a title in its title

Eco, Umberto. Postscript to The Name of the Rose. Trans. William Weaver. New York: Harcourt, 1983.

When a book's title contains another book title (as here: The Name of the Rose), do not underline the second title. When a book's title contains a quotation or the title of a work normally placed in quotation marks, keep the quotation marks and underline both titles: Critical Response to Henry James's "Beast in the Jungle." (Note that the underlining extends under the closing quotation mark.)

14. A work in more than one volume

Lincoln, Abraham. The Collected Works of Abraham Lincoln. Ed. Roy P. Basler. 8 vols. New Brunswick: Rutgers UP, 1953.

Lincoln, Abraham. The Collected Works of Abraham Lincoln. Ed. Roy P. Basler. Vol. 5. New Brunswick: Rutgers UP, 1953. 8 vols.

If you use two or more volumes of a multivolume work, give the work's total number of volumes before the publication information ("8 vols." in the first example). Your text citation will indicate which volume you are citing (see p. 8). If you use only one volume, give that volume number before the publication information ("Vol. 5" in the second example). You may add the total number of volumes to the end of the entry ("8 vols." in the second example).

If you cite a multivolume work published over a period of years, give the inclusive years as the publication date: for instance, Cambridge: Harvard UP, 1978-90.

15. A work in a series

Bergman, Ingmar. The Seventh Seal. Mod. Film Scripts Ser. 12. New York: Simon, 1968.

Place the name of the series (not quoted or underlined) just before the publication information. Abbreviate common words such as *modern* and *series*. Add any series number after the series title.

16. Published proceedings of a conference

Watching Our Language: A Conference Sponsored by the Program in Architecture and Design Criticism. 6-8 May 1999. New York: Parsons School of Design, 1999.

Whether in or after the title of the conference, supply information about who sponsored the conference, when it was held, and who published the proceedings. Treat a particular presentation at the conference like a selection from an anthology (model 18).

17. An anthology

Barnet, Sylvan, et al., eds. An Introduction to Literature. 11th ed. New York: Longman, 1997.

When citing an entire anthology, give the name of the editor or editors (followed by "ed." or "eds.") and then the title of the anthology. This anthology has four editors, so "et al." can replace all but the first editor's name. See model 3, page 16.

18. A selection from an anthology

Chekhov, Anton. "Misery." Trans. Constance Garnett. An Introduction to Literature. Ed. Sylvan Barnet et al. 11th ed. New York: Longman, 1997. 58-61.

The essentials of this listing are these: author of selection; title of selection (in quotation marks); title of anthology (underlined); editors' names preceded by "Ed." (meaning "Edited by"); publication information for the anthology; and inclusive page numbers for the selection (without the abbreviation "pp."). In addition, this source requires a translator for the selection and an edition number for the anthology. If you wish, you may also supply the original date of publication for the work you are citing, after its title. See model 12 on page 18.

If the work you cite comes from a collection of works by one author and with no editor, use the following form:

> Auden, W. H. "Family Ghosts." The Collected Poetry of W. H. Auden. New York: Random, 1945. 132-33.

If the work you cite is a scholarly article that was previously printed elsewhere, provide the complete information for the earlier publication of the piece, followed by "Rpt. in" ("Reprinted in") and the information for the source in which you found the piece:

> Reekmans, Tony. "Juvenal on Social Change." Ancient Society 2 (1971): 117-61. Rpt. in Private Life in Rome. Ed. Helen West. Los Angeles: Coronado, 1981. 124-69.

19. Two or more selections from the same anthology

> Auden, W. H. "The Unknown Citizen." Barnet et al. 687-88.
>
> Barnet, Sylvan, et al., eds. An Introduction to Literature. 11th ed. New York: Longman, 1997.
>
> Miller, Arthur. Death of a Salesman. Barnet et al. 1163-231.

When citing more than one selection from the same source, you may avoid repetition by giving the source in full (as in the Barnet et al. entry) and then simply cross-referencing it in entries for the works you used. Thus, instead of full information for the Auden and Miller works, give "Barnet et al." and the appropriate pages in that book. Note that each entry appears in its proper alphabetical place among other works cited.

20. An introduction, preface, foreword, or afterword

> Donaldson, Norman. Introduction. The Claverings. By Anthony Trollope. New York: Dover, 1977. vii-xv.

An introduction, foreword, or afterword is often written by someone other than the book's author. When citing such a piece, give its name without quotation marks or underlining. (But if the work has a title of its own, provide it, in quotation marks, between the name of the author and the name of the piece.) Follow the title of the book with its author's name preceded by "By." Give the inclusive page numbers of the part you cite. (In the preceding example, the small Roman numerals indicate that the cited work is in the front matter of the book, before page 1.)

When the author of a preface or introduction is the same as the author of the book, give only the last name after the title:

> Gould, Stephen Jay. Prologue. The Flamingo's Smile: Reflections in Natural History. By Gould. New York: Norton, 1985. 13-20.

21. An article in a reference work

> Mark, Herman F. "Polymers." The New Encyclopaedia Britannica: Macropaedia. 15th ed. 1991.
>
> "Reckon." Merriam-Webster's Collegiate Dictionary. 10th ed. 1998.

List an article in a reference work by its title (second example) unless the article is signed (first example). For works with entries arranged alphabetically, you need not include volume or page numbers. For well-known works like those listed above, you may also omit the editors' names and all publication information except any edition number and the year of publication. For works that are not well known, give full publication information:

> "Hungarians in America." The Ethnic Almanac. Ed. Stephanie Bernardo. New York: Doubleday, 1991. 109-11.

2 Listing periodicals: Journals, magazines, and newspapers

The basic format for an article from a periodical includes the following information:

> ① Lever, Janet. ② "Sex Differences in the Games Children Play." ③ Social Problems 23 (1976): 478-87.
>
> ⓐ ⓑ ⓒ ⓓ

1. *Author.* Use the author's full name: last name first, followed by a comma, and then the first name and any middle name or initial. Omit any title or degree attached to the author's name on the source, such as Dr. or Ph.D. End the name with a period and one space.
2. *Title of the article.* Give the full title, including any subtitle. Place the title in quotation marks, capitalize all important words in the title, and end the title with a period (inside the final quotation mark) and one space.

3. *Publication information.*
   a. The title of the periodical, underlined, followed by a space. Omit any *A*, *An*, or *The* from the beginning of the title.
   b. The volume and/or issue number (in Arabic numerals), followed by a space. See the note following.
   c. The date of publication, followed by a colon and a space. See the note following.
   d. The inclusive page numbers of the article (without the abbreviation "pp."). For the second number in inclusive page numbers over 100, provide only as many digits as needed for clarity (usually two): 87–88, 100–01, 398–401, 1026–36, 1190–206. If the article does not run on consecutive pages, provide only the first page number followed by a plus sign: 16+. (See also model 26, opposite.)

Note The treatment of volume and issue numbers and publication dates varies depending on the kind of periodical being cited, as the models indicate.

22. An article in a journal with continuous pagination throughout the annual volume

Lever, Janet. "Sex Differences in the Games Children Play." Social Problems 23 (1976): 478-87.

Some journals number the pages of issues consecutively throughout a year, so that each issue after the first in a year begins numbering where the previous issue left off—say, at page 132 or 416. For this kind of journal, give the volume number after the title ("23" in the example above) and place the year of publication in parentheses. The page numbers will be enough to guide readers to the appropriate issue.

23. An article in a journal that pages issues separately or that numbers only issues, not volumes

Dacey, June. "Management Participation in Corporate Buy-Outs." Management Perspectives 7.4 (1998): 20-31.

Some journals page each issue separately (starting each issue at page 1). For these journals, give the volume number, a period, and the issue number (as in "7.4" in the Dacey entry above). Then readers know which issue of the periodical to consult. When citing an article in a journal that numbers only issues, not annual volumes, treat the issue number as if it were a volume number, as in model 22.

24. An article in a monthly or bimonthly magazine

Tilin, Andrew. "Selling the Dream." Worth Oct. 1999: 94-100.

Follow the magazine title with the month and the year of publication. (Abbreviate all months except May, June, and July.) Don't place the date in parentheses, and don't provide a volume or issue number.

25. An article in a weekly or biweekly magazine

Stevens, Mark. "Low and Behold." New Republic 24 Dec. 1990: 27-33.

Follow the magazine title with the day, the month (abbreviated), and the year of publication. (Abbreviate all months except May, June, and July.) Don't place the date in parentheses, and don't provide a volume or issue number.

26. An article in a daily newspaper

Lewis, Peter H. "Many Updates Cause Profitable Confusion." New York Times 21 Jan. 1999, natl. ed.: D1+.

Give the name of the newspaper as it appears on the first page (but without *A*, *An*, or *The*). If the name of the city is not in the title of a local newspaper, add the city name in brackets after the title, without underlining: Gazette [Chicago]. Then follow model 25, with two differences: (1) If the newspaper lists an edition at the top of the first page, include that information after the date and a comma. (See "natl. ed." above.) (2) If the newspaper is divided into lettered or numbered sections, provide the section designation before the page number when the newspaper does the same (as in "D1+" above); otherwise, provide the section designation before the colon—for instance, sec. 1: 1+. The plus sign here and with "D1+" in the preceding model indicates that the articles do not run on consecutive pages but start on page 1 or D1 and continue later.

27. An unsigned article

"The Right to Die." Time 11 Oct. 1976: 101.

Begin the entry for an unsigned article with the title of the article. In the list of works cited, alphabetize an anonymous source by the first main word of the title ("Right" in this model).

28. An editorial or letter to the editor

"Bodily Intrusions." Editorial. New York Times 29 Aug. 1990, late ed.: A20.

Add the word "Editorial" or "Letter"—but without quotation marks—after the title if there is one or after the author's name, as follows:

Dowding, Michael. Letter. Economist 5-11 Jan. 1985: 4.

(The numbers "5-11" in this entry are the publication days of the periodical: the issue spans January 5 through 11.)

29. A review

Dunne, John Gregory. "The Secret of Danny Santiago." Rev. of Famous All over Town, by Danny Santiago. New York Review of Books 16 Aug. 1984: 17-27.

"Rev." is an abbreviation for "Review." The name of the author of the work being reviewed follows the title of the work, a comma, and "by." If the review has no title of its own, then "Rev. of . . ." (without quotation marks) immediately follows the name of the reviewer.

30. An abstract of a dissertation or article

Steciw, Steven K. "Alterations to the Pessac Project of Le Corbusier." Diss. U of Cambridge, England, 1986. DAI 46 (1986): 565C.

For an abstract appearing in *Dissertation Abstracts* (*DA*) or *Dissertation Abstracts International* (*DAI*), give the author's name and the title, "Diss." (for "Dissertation"), the institution granting the author's degree, the date of the dissertation, and the publication information.

For an abstract of an article, first provide the publication information for the article itself, followed by the information for the abstract. If the abstract publisher lists abstracts by item rather than page number, add "item" before the number.

Lever, Janet "Sex Differences in the Games Children Play." Social Problems 23 (1976): 478-87. Psychological Abstracts 63 (1976): item 1431.

3 Listing electronic sources

Electronic sources include those available on CD-ROM and those available online, such as through the Internet. Like citations of print sources, citations of online sources require available information such as author, title, and date of publication (date of online posting or last revision for an online source). But online sources also require two special pieces of information:

- Give the date when you consulted the source as well as the date when the source was posted or updated online. The posting date comes first, with other publication information. Your access date falls near the end of the entry, just before the electronic address.
- Give the source's exact electronic address, enclosed in angle brackets (<>). Usually, you'll find the address in your Web browser's Location or Address field near the top of the screen

as you're viewing the source. (Be sure to give the complete address for the specific page you are using, not just for the site's home page.) Place the address at the end of the entry. If you must break an address from one line to the next, do so *only* after a slash, and do not hyphenate.

Try to locate all the information required in the following models, referring to pages 3–4 for help. However, if you search for and still cannot find some information, then give what you can find.

Note You can supplement or replace MLA style for online sources with Columbia online style (Chapter 6). However, there are differences between the two styles (described on pp. 70–71), so ask your instructor which one you should use.

31. A source on a periodical CD-ROM

A source also published in print:

Lewis, Peter H. "Many Updates Cause Profitable Confusion." New York Times 21 Jan. 1999, natl. ed.: D1+. New York Times Ondisc. CD-ROM. UMI-ProQuest. Mar. 1999.

If you cite a source on CD-ROM that's issued periodically (like a journal or magazine), look for information about a print version of the same source. (The information is usually at the beginning of the source.) If there is such information, provide it as in the model above (1), referring to pages 22–24 as needed. Then provide the following information on the CD-ROM version: the title of the CD-ROM (2), underlined; the medium, "CD-ROM" (3), without quotation marks or underlining; the name of the vendor (or distributor) of the CD-ROM (4); and the date of electronic publication (5).

A periodical CD-ROM without information for a print version:

"Vanguard Forecasts." Business Outlook. CD-ROM. Information Access. Mar. 1999.

If a periodical source appears only on CD-ROM (not also in print), give only the CD-ROM title, the medium, the vendor, and the date.

32. A source on a nonperiodical CD-ROM

Shelley, Mary Wollstonecraft. Frankenstein. Classic Library. CD-ROM. Alameda: Andromeda, 1993.

If you cite a single-issue CD-ROM, first provide its author (1) and title (2). Underline titles of books or similarly long works; use quotation marks for short works such as stories or parts of books. Then give the underlined title of the entire disk (3), if there is a title; give the medium (4), without quotation marks or underlining; and end with the disk's place of publication, publisher, and date of publication (5).

If the work you cite or the entire disk has a version or edition number, add it at the appropriate place, as shown in the model below:

> "Sugar." Concise Columbia Encyclopedia. 3rd ed. Microsoft Bookshelf. CD-ROM. 1998-99 ed. Redmond: Microsoft, 1998.

This model also shows citation of a part of a work (in quotation marks) with no author.

33. An online book

A book published independently:

> James, Henry. The Turn of the Screw. New York: Scribner's, 1908-09. 4 Mar. 1999 <http://www.americanliterature.com/TS/TSINDX.HTML>.

For an online book published independently, not as part of a scholarly project or other larger site, provide the author's name (1); the underlined title of the book (2); any publication information for the original print version of the book (3); the date you consulted the source (4); and the electronic address (5). If the book was not published in print before, substitute the date of electronic publication for the print publication information. If the book has an editor or translator, include that information as in the following model.

A book within a scholarly project:

> Austen, Jane. Emma. Ed. Ronald Blythe. Harmondsworth: Penguin, 1972. Oxford Text Archive. 1994. Oxford U. 15 Dec. 1997 <ftp://ota.ox.ac.uk/pub/ota/public/english/Austen/emma.1519>.

For a book published as part of a scholarly project, first list the author and title (1), the name of any editor or translator (2), and any print publication information provided in the source (3). Add the title of the project (4), underlined; the date of electronic publication (5); the name of any sponsoring organization or institution (6); the date of your access (7); and the electronic address (8), which should direct readers to the book rather than to the project as a whole. If the project has an editor, add the name after the project's title (see model 39 on p. 28).

34. An article in an online journal

Palfrey, Andrew. "Choice of Mates in Identical Twins." Modern Psychology 4.1 (1996): 12 pars. 25 Feb. 2000 <http://www.liasu.edu/modpsy/palfrey4(1).htm>.

Follow model 22 or 23 on page 22 for citing a scholarly article (1), but add the date you consulted the source (2) and the electronic address (3). If the journal provides page, paragraph, or other reference numbers, give the inclusive numbers (such as 20-31 for pages, as in model 23) or the total number (such as 12 pars. in the model above). Omit reference numbers if the source does not use them.

35. An online abstract

Palfrey, Andrew. "Choice of Mates in Identical Twins." Modern Psychology 4.1 (1996): 12 pars. Abstract. 25 Feb. 2000 <http://www.liasu.edu/modpsy/abstractpalfrey4(1).htm>.

Treat an online abstract like an online journal article (model 34 above), but add "Abstract" (without quotation marks or underlining) between the publication information and the date of your access.

36. An article in an online newspaper

Still, Lucia. "On the Battlefields of Business, Millions of Casualties." New York Times on the Web 3 Mar. 1999. 17 Aug. 1999 <http://www.nytimes.com/specials/downsize/03down1.html>.

For an online newspaper article, provide the author's name (1); the title of the article (2), in quotation marks; the title of the online newspaper (3), underlined; the date of publication (4); the date you consulted the source (5); and the electronic address for the article (6). Provide section, page, or paragraph numbers if the newspaper does, as in model 26 (p. 23).

37. An article in an online magazine

Palevitz, Barry A., and Ricki Lewis. "Death Raises Safety Issues for Primate Handlers." Scientist 2 Mar. 1998: 1+. 27 Mar. 1998 <http://www.the-scientist.library.upenn.edu/yr1998/mar/palevitz_pl_980302.html>.

Cite an article in an online magazine with the name(s) of the author(s) (1); the title of the article (2), in quotation marks; the title of the periodical (3), underlined; the date of publication (4); any page, paragraph, or other reference numbers (5); the date you consulted the source (6); and the electronic address (7).

38. An online review

Detwiler, Donald S., and Chu Shao-Kang. Rev. of Important Documents of the Republic of China, ed. Tan Quon Chin. Journal of Military History 56.4 (1992): 669-84. 16 Sept. 1997 <http://www.jstor.org/fcgi-bin/jstor/viewitem.fcg/08993718/96p0008x>.

Cite an online review following model 29 on page 24 and the appropriate model on the previous page for an online scholarly journal, newspaper, or magazine (1). Include the date you consulted the source (2) and the electronic address (3).

39. An online scholarly project or database

Scots Teaching and Research Network. Ed. John Corbett. 2 Feb. 1998. U of Glasgow. 5 Mar. 1999 <http://www.arts.gla.ac.uk/www/english/comet/starn/htm>.

When citing an entire project or database, provide the title (1), underlined; the name of any editor (2); the date of publication (3); the name of any organization or institution that sponsors the project or database (4); the date you consulted the source (5); and the electronic address (6). If the project or database has a version number, add it after the editor's name and before the date of publication—for instance, Vers. 3.2.

40. A short work from an online scholarly project or database

Barbour, John. "The Brus." Scots Teaching and Research Network. Ed. John Corbett. 2 Feb. 1998. U of Glasgow. 5 Mar. 1999 <http://www.arts.gla.ac.uk/www/english/comet/starn/poetry/brus/contents/htm>.

For a poem, an article, or another short work published as part of a scholarly project or database, start with the author's name (1) and the title of the short work (2), in quotation marks. Then follow the model above for the complete project (3), but give the specific electronic address for the short work (4).

41. A personal or professional online site

> Lederman, Leon. Topics in Modern Physics--Lederman. 12 Dec. 1999 <http://www-ed.fnal.gov/samplers/hsphys/people/lederman.html>.

Cite a personal or professional site with the author's name (1); the title if any (2), underlined; the date you consulted the source (3); and the electronic address (4). If the source has no title, describe it with a label such as "Home page," without quotation marks or underlining. If it has a sponsoring organization or institution, add the name after the title.

42. A work from an online subscription service

> Wilkins, Johanna M. "The Myths of the Only Child." Psychology Update 12 Dec. 1999: 16-20. ProQuest Health and Medical Complete. ProQuest Direct. Manhattan Community Coll. Lib., New York. 20 Dec. 1999 <http://www.umi.com/proquest/>.

Online subscription services include those your library subscribes to (such as ProQuest Direct or Lexis-Nexis) and those you subscribe to yourself (such as America Online). If the service you use gives a specific electronic address for your source, you can generally base your works-cited entry on models 33–41, selecting the one that matches your kind of source. However, if the service does not provide the source's specific address, then you need to follow the model above or the one below. The model above, for a library service, begins with author, title, and publication information as appropriate for a magazine article (1). It then adds the name of the database (2), underlined; the name of the service (3), not underlined; the name and location of the subscribing library (4); the date of access (5); and the electronic address of the service's home page (6). You can omit item 2 or 6 if you don't have the information.

Some subscription services ask users to search with keywords or through a directory (or path) of topics:

> "China--Dragon Kings." The Encyclopedia Mythica. America Online. 6 Jan. 1999. Path: Research and Learn; Encyclopedia; More Encyclopedias; Encyclopedia Mythica.

This model includes the title of the source and the larger work (1), the name of the service (2), the date of access (3), and then "Path:" (without quotation marks or underlining) and the sequence of topics required to reach the source (4), with the topics separated by semicolons.

If you reached the source with a keyword rather than a path, give that information instead—for instance, Keyword: Mythica.

43. Electronic mail

Millon, Michele. "Re: Grief Therapy." E-mail to the author.
4 May 1997.

For e-mail, give the name of the writer (1); the title, if any, from the e-mail's subject heading (2), in quotation marks; a description of the transmission, including whom it was sent to (3); and the date of posting (4).

44. A posting to a discussion list

The original posting:

Tourville, Michael. "European Currency Reform." Online posting.
6 Jan. 1999. International Finance Discussion List.
12 Jan. 1999 <finance-dl@weg.isu.edu>.

For a list subscribed to via e-mail, give the author's name (1); the title, if any, from the e-mail's subject heading (2), in quotation marks; the words "Online posting" (3), without quotation marks or underlining; the date of the posting (4); the name of the list (5); the date you consulted the source (6); and the electronic address (7).

An archived posting:

Tourville, Michael. "European Currency Reform." Online posting.
6 Jan. 1999. International Finance Archive. 2 June 1999
<http://www.weg.isu.edu/finance-dl/46732>.

Whenever possible, cite an archived version of the posting. If the posting has an identifying number, insert it immediately after the list's name—for example, Art Finds Discussion List 22634.

45. A posting to a newsgroup or Web forum

A newsgroup:

Cramer, Sherry. "Recent Investment Practices in U.S. Business."

Online posting. 26 Mar. 2000. 3 Apr. 2000
<news:biz.investment.current.2700>.

A newsgroup is not subscriber-based. For a posting to a newsgroup, give the author's name (1); the title from the subject heading (2), in quotation marks; "Online posting" (3), without quotation marks or underlining; the date of posting (4); the date you consulted the source (5); and, in angle brackets, the group's name preceded by "news:" (6), as in the example.

A Web forum:

Franklin, Melanie. Online posting. 25 Jan. 1999. The Creative
Process: An Artist's Diary. 27 Jan. 1999 <http://forums/
nytimes/com/webin/WebX?14@^182943@eea7>

Give the author (1); the title, if any, in quotation marks (the example has no title); "Online posting" (2), without quotation marks or underlining; the date of posting (3); the name of the forum (4); the date of your access (5); and the address (6).

46. An online graphic, video, or audio file

Hamilton, Calvin J. "Components of Comets." Diagram. Space Art.
1997. 20 Dec. 1999 <wysisiwyg://94/http://spaceart.com/
solar/eng/comet.htm>.

In general, you can base citations of online visual or audio sources on models 52–56 and 60 (pp. 33–34, 36), adding information appropriate for an online source. This example includes the creator's name (1); the title of the source (2); a description of the source (3), without quotation marks or underlining; the title of the larger work in which the source appears (4), underlined; the date of the source (5); the date of access (6); and the electronic address (7).

47. A synchronous communication (MUD, MOO, etc.)

Bruckman, Amy. MediaMOO Symposium: Virtual Worlds for
Business? 20 Jan. 1998. MediaMOO. 26 Feb. 1998 <http://
www.cc.gatech.edu/fac/Amy.Bruckman/MediaMOO/
cscw-symposium-98.html>.

Cite a synchronous communication with the name of the speaker (1); a description of the event (2), without quotation marks or underlining; the date of the event (3); the forum (4); the date you consulted the source (5); and the electronic address (6). Whenever possible, cite an archived version of the communication (see model 44 on p. 30).

48. Computer software

① ② ③

Project Scheduler 8000. Vers. 4.1. Orlando: Scitor, 1999.

For software, provide the title (1), underlined; the version number (2); and the publication information (3), including place of publication, publisher, and date. If you consulted or obtained the software online, replace this publication information with the date of your access and the electronic address, as in previous examples.

4 Listing other sources

49. A government publication

Hawaii. Dept. of Education. Kauai District Schools, Profile 1996-97. Honolulu: Hawaii Dept. of Education, 1998.

Stiller, Ann. Historic Preservation and Tax Incentives. US Dept. of Interior. Washington: GPO, 1996.

United States. Cong. House. Committee on Ways and Means. Medicare Payment for Outpatient Occupational Therapy Services. 102nd Cong., 1st sess. Washington: GPO, 1991.

If an author is not listed for a government publication, give the appropriate agency as author, as in the first and last examples. Provide information in the order illustrated, separating elements with a period and a space: the name of the government, the name of the agency (which may be abbreviated), and the title and publication information. For a congressional publication (last example), give the house and committee involved before the title, and give the number and session of Congress after the title. In the second and last examples, "GPO" stands for the US Government Printing Office.

50. A pamphlet

Medical Answers About AIDS. New York: Gay Men's Health Crisis, 1998.

Most pamphlets can be treated as books. In the example above, the pamphlet has no listed author, so the title comes first. If the pamphlet has an author, list his or her name first, followed by the title and publication information as given here.

51. An unpublished dissertation or thesis

Wilson, Stuart M. "John Stuart Mill as a Literary Critic." Diss. U of Michigan, 1970.

The title is quoted rather than underlined. "Diss." stands for "Dissertation." "U of Michigan" is the institution that granted the author's degree.

52. A musical composition or work of art

Fauré, Gabriel. Sonata for Violin and Piano no. 1 in A major, op. 15.

Don't underline musical compositions identified only by form, number, and key. Do underline titled operas, ballets, and compositions (Carmen, Sleeping Beauty).

For a work of art, underline the title and include the name and location of the owner. For a work you see only in a photograph, provide the complete publication information, too, as in the following model. Omit such information only if you examined the actual work.

Sargent, John Singer. Venetian Doorway. Metropolitan Museum of Art, New York. Sargent Watercolors. By Donelson F. Hoopes. New York: Watson, 1976. 31.

53. A film or video recording

Schindler's List. Dir. Steven Spielberg. Perf. Liam Neeson and Ben Kingsley. Universal, 1993.

Start with the title of the work you are citing, unless you are citing the contribution of a particular individual (see the next model). Give additional information (writer, lead performers, and so on) as you judge appropriate. For a film, end with the distributor and date.

For a videocassette, filmstrip, or slide program, include the original release date (if any) and the medium (without underlining or quotation marks) before the distributor's name:

George Balanchine, chor. Serenade. Perf. San Francisco Ballet. Dir. Hilary Bean. 1981. Videocassette. PBS Video, 1987.

54. A television or radio program

Kenyon, Jane, and Donald Hall. "A Life Together." Bill Moyers' Journal. PBS. WNET, New York. 17 Dec. 1998.

As in model 53, start with a title unless you are citing the work of a person or persons. The example above begins with the participants' names, then the episode title (in quotation marks), then the program title (underlined). Finish the entry with the name of the network, the local station and city, and the date.

55. A performance

The English Only Restaurant. By Silvio Martinez Palau. Dir. Susana Tubert. Puerto Rican Traveling Theater, New York. 27 July 1999.

Ozawa, Seiji, cond. Boston Symphony Orch. Symphony Hall, Boston. 25 Apr. 1997.

As with films and television programs, place the title first unless you are citing the work of an individual (second example). Provide additional information about participants after the title, as well as the theater, city, and date. Note that the orchestra name in the second example is neither quoted nor underlined.

56. A recording

Siberry, Jane. "Caravan." Maria. Reprise, 1995.

Brahms, Johannes. Concerto no. 2 in B-flat, op. 83. Perf. Artur Rubinstein. Cond. Eugene Ormandy. Philadelphia Orch. LP. RCA, 1972.

Begin with the name of the individual whose work you are citing. If you're citing a song, give the title in quotation marks. Then provide the title of the recording, underlining the title (first example) unless it identifies a composition by form, number, and key (second example). After the title, provide the names of any other artists it seems appropriate to mention, the manufacturer of the recording, and the date of release. If the medium is other than compact disk, provide it immediately before the manufacturer's name—for instance, LP (as in the second example) or Audiocassette.

57. A letter

Buttolph, Mrs. Laura E. Letter to Rev. and Mrs. C. C. Jones. 20 June 1857. In The Children of Pride: A True Story of Georgia and the Civil War. Ed. Robert Manson Myers. New Haven: Yale UP, 1972. 334-35.

A published letter is listed under the writer's name. Specify that the source is a letter and to whom it was addressed, and give the date on which it was written. Treat the remaining information like that for a selection from an anthology (model 18, p. 19). (See also p. 23 for the format of a letter to the editor of a periodical.)

For a letter in the collection of a library or archive, specify the writer, recipient, and date, as above, and give the name and location of the archive as well:

James, Jonathan E. Letter to his sister. 16 Apr. 1970. Jonathan E. James Papers. South Dakota State Archive, Pierre.

For a letter you receive, give the name of the writer, note the fact that the letter was sent to you, and provide the date of the letter:

Packer, Ann E. Letter to the author. 15 June 1999.

Use the form above for personal electronic mail (e-mail) as well, substituting "E-mail" for "Letter": E-mail to the author (see p. 30).

58. A lecture or address

Carlone, Dennis. "Architecture for the City of the Twenty-First Century." Tenth Symposium on Urban Issues. Cambridge City Hall, Cambridge. 22 May 2000.

Give the speaker's name, the title (in quotation marks), the title of the meeting, the name of the sponsoring organization, the location of the lecture, and the date. If you do not know the title, replace it with "Lecture" or another description, but *not* in quotation marks.

Although the *MLA Handbook* does not provide a specific style for classroom lectures in your courses, you can adapt the preceding format for this purpose:

Ezzy, T. G. Class lectures on the realist novel. Dawson College. 20 Jan. 1999-13 May 1999.

A parenthetical text citation to a particular lecture would require a date: (Ezzy, 12 Mar. 1999).

59. An interview

Graaf, Vera. Personal interview. 19 Dec. 1999.

Christopher, Warren. Interview. Frontline. PBS. WGBH, Boston. 13 Feb. 1998.

Begin with the name of the person interviewed. For an interview you conducted, specify "Personal interview" or the medium (such as "Telephone interview" or "E-mail interview")—without quotation marks or underlining—and then give the date. For an interview you read, heard, or saw, provide the title if any or "Interview" if not, along with other bibliographic information and the date.

60. A map or other illustration

Women in the Armed Forces. Map. Women in the World: An International Atlas. By Joni Seager and Ann Olson. New York: Touchstone, 1999. 44-45.

List the illustration by its title (underlined). Provide a descriptive label ("Map," "Chart," "Table"), without underlining or quotation marks, and the publication information. If the creator of the illustration is credited in the source, put his or her name first in the entry, as with any author.

CHAPTER 3

CMS Style

3a Citing sources in the humanities: Chicago style

Writers in the humanities generally rely on one of the following guides for source-citation style:

The Chicago Manual of Style. 14th ed. 1993.
Gibaldi, Joseph. *MLA Handbook for Writers of Research Papers.* 5th ed. 1999.
Turabian, Kate L. *A Manual for Writers of Term Papers, Theses, and Dissertations.* 6th ed. Rev. John Grossman and Alice Bennett. 1996.

The recommendations of the *MLA Handbook,* discussed in Chapter 2, are usually used for papers in English and foreign languages. In history, art history, and many other disciplines, however, writers rely on *The Chicago Manual* or the student reference adapted from it, *A Manual for Writers.*

Both books detail two documentation styles. One, used mainly by scientists and social scientists, closely resembles the style of the American Psychological Association, covered in Chapter 4. The other style, used more in the humanities, calls for footnotes or endnotes and an optional bibliography. This style is described below.

1 Using Chicago notes and a list of works cited

In the Chicago note style, a raised numeral in the text refers the reader to endnotes or footnotes. The first citation of each source contains all the information readers need to find the source. Thus your instructor may consider a list of works cited optional.

Use single spacing for each note and double spacing between notes. Separate footnotes from the text with a short line above the

http://www.press.uchicago.edu/Misc/Chicago/cmosfaq.html Answers to frequently asked questions about Chicago style, from the University of Chicago Press.

first note. With endnotes, use the format below for a list of works cited, substituting the heading "NOTES" and numbered entries as for footnotes.

For the list of sources at the end of the paper, use the format below. Arrange the sources alphabetically by the authors' last names.

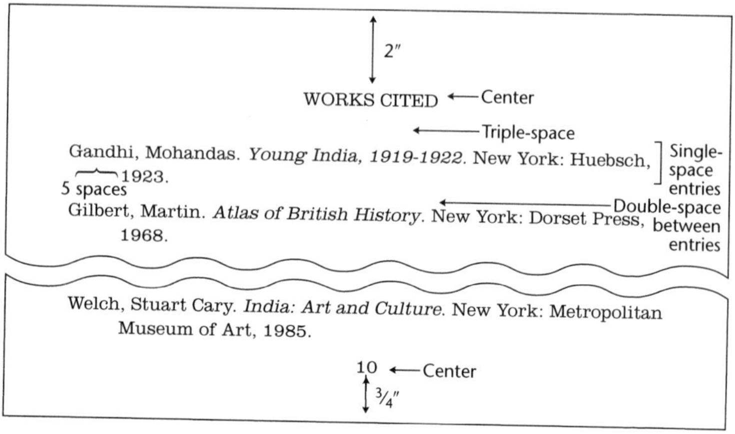

The examples below illustrate the essentials of a note and a works-cited entry.

Note

6. Martin Gilbert, *Atlas of British History* (New York: Dorset Press, 1968), 96.

Works-cited entry

Gilbert, Martin. *Atlas of British History*. New York: Dorset Press, 1968.

Notes and works-cited entries share certain features:

- Italicize or underline the titles of books and periodicals (ask your instructor for his or her preference).
- Enclose in quotation marks the titles of parts of books or articles in periodicals.
- Do not abbreviate publishers' names, but omit "Inc.," "Co.," and similar abbreviations.
- Do not use "p." or "pp." before page numbers.

Notes and works-cited entries also differ in important ways:

Note	Works-cited entry
Start with a number (typed on the line and followed by a period) that corresponds to the note number in the text.	Do not begin with a number.
Indent the first line five spaces.	Indent the second and subsequent lines five spaces.

Note	Works-cited entry
Give the author's name in normal order.	Begin with the author's last name.
Use commas between elements such as author's name and title.	Use periods between elements, followed by one space.
Enclose publication information in parentheses, with no preceding punctuation.	Precede the publication information with a period, and don't use parentheses.
Include the specific page number(s) you borrowed from, omitting "p." or "pp."	Omit page numbers except for parts of books or articles in periodicals.

Many computerized word-processing programs will automatically position footnotes at the bottoms of appropriate pages. Some will automatically number notes and renumber them if you add or delete one or more.

2 Following Chicago models

In these models for common sources, notes and works-cited entries appear together for easy reference. Be sure to use the numbered note form for notes and the unnumbered works-cited form for works-cited entries.

Books

1. A book with one, two, or three authors

1. Carol Gilligan, *In a Different Voice: Psychological Theory and Women's Development* (Cambridge: Harvard University Press, 1982), 27.

Gilligan, Carol. *In a Different Voice: Psychological Theory and Women's Development.* Cambridge: Harvard University Press, 1982.

1. Dennis L. Wilcox, Phillip H. Ault, and Warren K. Agee, *Public Relations: Strategies and Tactics,* 4th ed. (New York: HarperCollins, 1995), 182.

Wilcox, Dennis L., Phillip H. Ault, and Warren K. Agee. *Public Relations: Strategies and Tactics.* 4th ed. New York: HarperCollins, 1995.

2. A book with more than three authors

2. Geraldo Lopez and others, *China and the West* (Boston: Little, Brown, 1990), 461.

Lopez, Geraldo, Judith P. Salt, Anne Ming, and Henry Reisen. *China and the West.* Boston: Little, Brown, 1990.

Chicago note and works-cited models

3. A book with an editor

3. Hendrick Ruitenbeek, ed., *Freud as We Knew Him* (Detroit: Wayne State University Press, 1973), 64.

Ruitenbeek, Hendrick, ed. *Freud as We Knew Him.* Detroit: Wayne State University Press, 1973.

4. A book with an author and an editor

4. Lewis Mumford, *The City in History,* ed. Donald L. Miller (New York: Pantheon, 1986), 216-17.

Mumford, Lewis. *The City in History.* Edited by Donald L. Miller. New York: Pantheon, 1986.

5. A translation

5. Dante Alighieri, *The Inferno,* trans. John Ciardi (New York: New American Library, 1971), 51.

Alighieri, Dante. *The Inferno.* Translated by John Ciardi. New York: New American Library, 1971.

6. An anonymous work

6. *The Dorling Kindersley World Reference Atlas* (London: Dorling Kindersley, 1994), 150-51.

The Dorling Kindersley World Reference Atlas. London: Dorling Kindersley, 1994.

7. A later edition

7. Dwight L. Bollinger, *Aspects of Language,* 2d ed. (New York: Harcourt Brace Jovanovich, 1975), 20.

Bollinger, Dwight L. *Aspects of Language.* 2d ed. New York: Harcourt Brace Jovanovich, 1975.

8. A work in more than one volume

Citation of one volume without a title:

8. Abraham. Lincoln, *The Collected Works of Abraham Lincoln,* ed. Roy P. Basler (New Brunswick: Rutgers University Press, 1953), 5:426-28.

Lincoln, Abraham. *The Collected Works of Abraham Lincoln.* Edited by Roy P. Basler. Vol. 5. New Brunswick: Rutgers University Press, 1953.

Citation of one volume with a title:

8. Linda B. Welkin, *The Age of Balanchine,* vol. 3 of *The History of Ballet* (New York: Columbia University Press, 1969), 56.

Welkin, Linda B. *The Age of Balanchine.* Vol. 3 of *The History of Ballet.* New York: Columbia University Press, 1969.

9. A selection from an anthology

9. Rosetta Brooks, "Streetwise," in *The New Urban Landscape,* ed. Richard Martin (New York: Rizzoli, 1990), 38-39.

Brooks, Rosetta. "Streetwise." In *The New Urban Landscape,* ed. Richard Martin, 37-60. New York: Rizzoli, 1990.

10. A work in a series

10. Ingmar Bergman, *The Seventh Seal,* Modern Film Scripts Series, no. 12 (New York: Simon and Schuster, 1968), 27.

Bergman, Ingmar. *The Seventh Seal.* Modern Film Scripts Series, no. 12. New York: Simon and Schuster, 1968.

11. An article in a reference work

The abbreviation "s.v." in the examples stands for the Latin *sub verbo,* "under the word."

11. *Merriam-Webster's Collegiate Dictionary,* 10th ed., s.v. "reckon."

Merriam-Webster's Collegiate Dictionary, 10th ed., s.v. "reckon."

11. Mark F. Herman, "Polymers," in *The New Encyclopaedia Britannica. Macropaedia,* 16th ed.

Herman, Mark F. "Polymers." In *The New Encyclopaedia Britannica: Macropaedia,* 16th ed.

Periodicals: Journals, magazines, newspapers

12. An article in a journal with continuous pagination throughout the annual volume

12. Janet Lever, "Sex Differences in the Games Children Play," *Social Problems* 23 (1976): 482.

Lever, Janet. "Sex Differences in the Games Children Play." *Social Problems* 23 (1976): 478-87.

13. An article in a journal that pages issues separately

13. June Dacey, "Management Participation in Corporate Buy-Outs," *Management Perspectives* 7, no. 4 (1998): 22.

Dacey, June. "Management Participation in Corporate Buy-Outs." *Management Perspectives* 7, no. 4 (1998): 20-31.

14. An article in a popular magazine

14. Mark Stevens, "Low and Behold," *New Republic,* 24 December 1990, 28.

Stevens, Mark. "Low and Behold." *New Republic,* 24 December 1990, 27-33.

15. An article in a newspaper

15. Peter H. Lewis, "Many Updates Cause Profitable Confusion," *New York Times,* 21 January 1999, national ed., D5.

Lewis, Peter H. "Many Updates Cause Profitable Confusion." *New York Times,* 21 January 1999, national ed., D1, D5.

16. A review

16. John Gregory Dunne, "The Secret of Danny Santiago," review of *Famous All over Town,* by Danny Santiago, *New York Review of Books,* 16 August 1984, 25.

Dunne, John Gregory. "The Secret of Danny Santiago." Review of *Famous All over Town,* by Danny Santiago. *New York Review of Books,* 16 August 1984, 17-27.

Electronic sources

The Chicago Manual offers some models for documenting electronic sources, and *A Manual for Writers* updates these and adds a few more. For other electronic sources and simpler formats, you can use Columbia online style for the humanities, discussed in Chapter 6. Page 71 shows how to adapt Columbia style to Chicago style and details the differences between the two styles. Ask your instructor which style you should use for online sources.

Note Since Chicago style does not specify how to break electronic addresses in notes and works-cited entries, follow MLA style: break only after slashes, and do not hyphenate.

17. A source on a periodical CD-ROM

A source also published in print:

17. Peter H. Lewis, "Many Updates Cause Profitable Confusion," *New York Times,* 21 January 1999, national ed., D5. *New York Times Ondisc* [CD-ROM], UMI-ProQuest, March 1999.

Lewis, Peter H. "Many Updates Cause Profitable Confusion." *New York Times,* 21 January 1999, national ed., D1, D5. *New York Times Ondisc* [CD-ROM]. UMI-ProQuest, March 1999.

A source not published in print:

17. "Vanguard Forecasts," *Business Outlook* [CD-ROM], Information Access, March 1998.

"Vanguard Forecasts." *Business Outlook* [CD-ROM]. Information Access, March 1998.

18. A source on a nonperiodical CD-ROM

18. Mary Wollstonecraft Shelley, *Frankenstein, Classic Library* [CD-ROM] (Alameda, Calif.: Andromeda, 1993).

Shelley, Mary Wollstonecraft. *Frankenstein. Classic Library* [CD-ROM]. Alameda, Calif.: Andromeda, 1993.

19. An online book

19. Jane Austen, *Emma* [book online], ed. Ronald Blythe (Harmondsworth, Eng.: Penguin, 1972, accessed 15 December 1999), *Oxford Text Archive;* available from ftp://ota.ox.ac.uk/public/english/Austen/emma.1519; Internet.

Austen, Jane. *Emma* [book online]. Edited by Ronald Blythe. Harmondsworth, Eng.: Penguin, 1972. Accessed 15 December 1999. *Oxford Text Archive.* Available from ftp://ota.ox.ac.uk/public/english/Austen/emma.1519; Internet.

20. An article in an online periodical

20. Andrew Palfrey, "Choice of Mates in Identical Twins," *Modern Psychology* 4, no. 1 (1996): par. 10 [journal online]; available from http://www.liasu.edu/modpsy/palfrey4(1).htm; Internet; accessed 25 February 2000.

Palfrey, Andrew. "Choice of Mates in Identical Twins." *Modern Psychology* 4, no. 1 (1996): 12 pars. [journal online]. Available from http://www.liasu.edu/modpsy/palfrey4(1).htm; Internet. Accessed 25 February 2000.

21. An online database

21. *Scots Teaching and Research Network* [database online], ed. John Corbett (Glasgow: University of Glasgow, 2 February 1998, accessed 5 March 1999); available from http://www.arts.gla.ac.uk/www/comet/starn.htm; Internet.

Scots Teaching and Research Network [database online]. Edited by John Corbett. Glasgow: University of Glasgow, 2 February 1998. Accessed 5 March 1999. Available from http://www.arts.gla.ac.uk/www/comet/starn.htm; Internet.

Other sources

22. A government publication

22. House, *Medicare Payment for Outpatient Physical and Occupational Therapy Services,* 102d Cong., 1st sess., 1991, H. Doc. 409, 12-13.

U.S. Congress. House. *Medicare Payment for Outpatient Physical and Occupational Therapy Services.* 102d Cong., 1st sess., 1991. H. Doc. 409.

23. A letter

A published letter:

23. Mrs. Laura E. Buttolph to Rev. and Mrs. C. C. Jones, 20 June 1857, *The Children of Pride: A True Story of Georgia and the Civil War,* ed. Robert Manson Myers (New Haven: Yale University Press, 1972), 334.

Buttolph, Mrs. Laura E. Letter to Rev. and Mrs. C. C. Jones, 20 June 1857. In *The Children of Pride; A True Story of Georgia and the Civil War,* ed. Robert Manson Myers. New Haven: Yale University Press, 1972.

A personal letter:

23. Ann E. Packer, letter to author, 15 June 1998.

Packer, Ann E. Letter to author. 15 June 1998.

24. An interview

24. Warren Christopher, interview by William Lindon, *Frontline,* Public Broadcasting System, 13 February 1998.

Christopher, Warren. Interview by William Lindon. *Frontline.* Public Broadcasting System, 13 February 1998.

25. A work of art

25. John Singer Sargent, *In Switzerland,* watercolor, 1908, Metropolitan Museum of Art, New York.

Sargent, John Singer. *In Switzerland,* watercolor, 1908. Metropolitan Museum of Art, New York.

26. A film or video recording

26. *Serenade,* George Balanchine, San Francisco Ballet, PBS Video, 1985, videocassette.

Serenade. George Balanchine. San Francisco Ballet. PBS Video, 1985. Videocassette.

27. A sound recording

27. Johannes Brahms, Concerto no. 2 in B-flat, Artur Rubinstein, Philadelphia Orchestra, Eugene Ormandy, RCA BRC4-6731, 1992.

Brahms, Johannes, Concerto no. 2 in B-flat. Artur Rubinstein. Philadelphia Orchestra. Eugene Ormandy. RCA BRC4-6731, 1992.

Two or more citations of the same source

To minimize clutter and give a quick sense of how often you cite a source, the Chicago style allows a shortened form for subsequent citations of a source you have already cited fully.

You may use the Latin abbreviation "ibid." (meaning "in the same place") to refer to the same source cited in the preceding note:

8. Janet Lever, "Sex Differences in the Games Children Play." *Social Problems* 23 (1976): 482.

9. Ibid., 483.

For any source already cited in your notes, not just immediately before, you may use the author's name and (if the author is responsible for more than one cited source) a shortened form of the title:

1. Carol Gilligan, *In a Different Voice: Psychological Theory and Women's Development* (Cambridge: Harvard University Press, 1982), 27.

2. Carol Gilligan, "Moral Development in the College Years," *The Modern American College,* ed. A. Chickering (San Francisco: Jossey-Bass, 1981), 286.

3. Gilligan, *In a Different Voice,* 47.

Omit the title if you are using only one source by the cited author.

The Chicago style recommends in-text parenthetical citations when you cite one or more works repeatedly. This practice allows you to avoid many notes saying "ibid." or giving the same author's name. In the example following, the note number refers to the complete source information in an endnote; the numbers in parentheses are page numbers in the same source.

British rule, observes Stuart Cary Welch, "seemed as permanent as Mount Everest."[7] Most Indians submitted, willingly or not, to British influence in every facet of life (423-24).

CHAPTER 4

APA Style

4a Citing sources in the social sciences: APA style

Some of the social sciences publish style guides that advise practitioners how to organize, document, and type papers. The following is a partial list:

American Anthropological Association. "Style Guide and Information for Authors." *American Anthropologist* (1977): 774–79.
American Political Science Association. *Style Manual for Political Science.* Rev. ed. 1993.
American Psychological Association. *Publication Manual of the American Psychological Association.* 4th ed. 1994.
American Sociological Association. "Editorial Guidelines." Inside front cover of each issue of *American Sociological Review.*
Columbia Law Review. *A Uniform System of Citation.* 16th ed. 1996.
Linguistic Society of America. "LSA Style Sheet." Printed every December in *LSA Bulletin.*

By far the most widely used style is that of the American Psychological Association (APA), so we detail it here. Always ask your instructor in any discipline what style you should use.

1 Using APA parenthetical text citations

In the APA documentation style, parenthetical citations within the text refer the reader to a list of sources at the end of the text. A parenthetical citation contains the author's last name, the date of publication, and sometimes the page number from which material is borrowed. See the next page for an index to the models for various kinds of sources.

http://www.apa.org/journals/acorner.html Answers to frequently asked questions about APA style, from the American Psychological Association.

http://owl.english.purdue.edu/Files/34.html Guidance on using APA style, from the Purdue Online Writing Lab.

APA parenthetical text citations

1. Author not named in your text

> One critic of Milgram's experiments insisted that the subjects "should have been fully informed of the possible effects on them" (Baumrind, 1968, p. 34).

When you do not name the author in your text, place in parentheses the author's name and the date of the source. The APA requires page number(s) preceded by "p." or "pp." for direct quotations (as in the example) and recommends them for paraphrases. Separate the elements with commas. Position the reference so that it is clear what material is being documented *and* so that the reference fits as smoothly as possible into your sentence structure. (See pp. 11–12 for guidelines.) The following would also be correct:

> In the view of one critic of Milgram's experiments (Baumrind, 1968), the subjects "should have been fully informed of the possible effects on them" (p. 34).

2. Author named in your text

> Baumrind (1968) insisted that the subjects in Milgram's study "should have been fully informed of the possible effects on them" (p. 34).

When you use the author's name in the text, do not repeat it in the reference. Place the reference next to the author's name. If you cite the same source again in the paragraph, you need not repeat the reference as long as it is clear that you are using the same source and the page number (if any) is the same. Here is a later sentence from the paragraph containing the preceding example:

> Baumrind also criticized the experimenters' rationale.

3. A work with two authors

> Pepinsky and DeStefano (1987) demonstrate that a teacher's language often reveals hidden biases.
>
> One study (Pepinsky & DeStefano, 1987) demonstrates the hidden biases often revealed in a teacher's language.

When given in the text, two authors' names are connected by "and." In a parenthetical citation, they are connected by an ampersand, "&."

4. A work with three to five authors

> Pepinsky, Dunn, Rentl, and Corson (1993) further demonstrate the biases evident in gestures.

In the first citation of a work with three to five authors, name all the authors, as in the example above.

In the second and subsequent references to a work with three to five authors, generally give only the first author's name, followed by "et al." (Latin for "and others"):

> In the work of Pepinsky et al. (1993), the loaded gestures include head shakes and eye contact.

However, two or more sources published in the same year could shorten to the same form—for instance, two references shortening to Pepinsky et al., 1993. In that case, cite the last names of as many authors as you need to distinguish the sources, and then give "et al.": for instance, (Pepinsky, Dunn, et al., 1993) and (Pepinsky, Bradley, et al., 1993).

5. A work with six or more authors

> One study (Rutter et al., 1996) attempts to explain these geographical differences in adolescent experience.

For six or more authors, even in the first citation of the work, give only the first author's name, followed by "et al." If two or more sources published in the same year shorten to the same form, give additional names as explained with model 4, above.

6. A work with a group author

> An earlier prediction was even more somber (Lorenz Research, 1997).

For a work that lists an institution, agency, corporation, or other group as author, treat the name of the group as if it were an individual's name.

7. An anonymous work

One article ("Right to Die," 1976) noted that a death-row inmate may crave notoriety.

For an anonymous or unsigned work, use the first two or three words of the title in place of an author's name, excluding an initial *The, A,* or *An.* Underline book and journal titles. Place quotation marks around article titles. (In the list of references, however, do not use quotation marks for article titles. See pp. 55–56.) Capitalize the significant words in all titles cited in the text. (But in the reference list, treat only periodical titles this way. See pp. 55–56.)

8. One of two or more works by the same author(s)

At about age seven, most children begin to use appropriate gestures to reinforce their stories (Gardner, 1973a).

When you cite one of two or more works by the same author(s), the date will tell readers which source you mean—as long as your reference list includes only one source published by the author(s) in that year. If your reference list includes two or more works published by the same author(s) *in the same year,* the works should be lettered in the reference list (see p. 54). Then your parenthetical citation should include the appropriate letter, as in "1973a" above.

9. Two or more works by different authors

Two studies (Herskowitz, 1994; Marconi & Hamblen, 1990) found that periodic safety instruction can dramatically reduce employees' accidents.

List the sources in alphabetical order by the first author's name. Insert a semicolon between sources.

10. An indirect source

Supporting data appear in a study by Wong (cited in Marconi & Hamblen, 1990).

The phrase "cited in" indicates that the reference to Wong's study was found in Marconi and Hamblen. Only Marconi and Hamblen then appears in the list of references.

11. An electronic source

Ferguson and Hawkins (1998) did not anticipate the "evident hostility" of participants (par. 6).

Electronic sources can be cited like printed sources, usually with the author's last name and the publication date. When quoting or paraphrasing electronic sources that number paragraphs instead of pages, provide that information in the text citation, substituting "par." (or "pars.") for "p." (or "pp."). If the source does not have numbering of any kind, provide just the author's name and the date.

2 Using an APA reference list

In APA style, the in-text parenthetical citations refer to the list of sources at the end of the text. This list, titled "References," includes full publication information on every source cited in the paper. The list falls at the end of the paper, numbered in sequence with the preceding pages.

The following sample shows the format of the first page of the APA reference list:

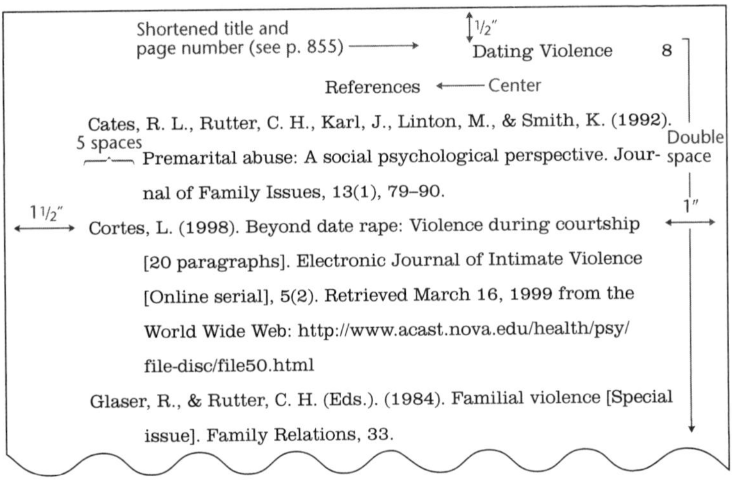

Arrangement

Arrange sources alphabetically by the author's last name or, if there is no author, by the first main word of the title.

Spacing

Double-space all entries.

Indention

Use an appropriate indention for each entry. For papers that will be published, the APA recommends indenting the first line of each entry five to seven spaces, as follows:

Rodriguez, R. (1982). A hunger of memory: The education of

Richard Rodriguez. Boston: Godine.

When set into type for publication, the initial indentions are then converted into so-called hanging indentions, in which the first line is not indented while the others are. The hanging indention makes it easier for readers to spot authors' names, so the APA recognizes that students who are preparing final copy (not destined for publication) may wish to use the hanging indention for their references, like so:

Rodriguez, R. (1982). A hunger of memory: The education of

Richard Rodriguez. Boston: Godine.

Because it is clearer for readers, the hanging indention is used in the sample on the previous page and in the following models for references, with a five-space indention for the second and subsequent lines of each entry.

Ask your instructor which format he or she prefers.

Punctuation

Separate the parts of the reference (author, date, title, and publication information) with a period and one space. Do not use a final period in references to electronic sources, which conclude with an electronic address (see pp. 56–58).

Authors

List all authors with last name first, separating names and parts of names with commas. Use initials for first and middle names. Use an ampersand (&) before the last author's name.

Publication date

Place the publication date in parentheses after the author's or authors' names, followed by a period. Generally, this date is the year only, though for some sources (such as magazine and newspaper articles) it includes month and sometimes day as well.

Titles

In titles of books and articles, capitalize only the first word of the title, the first word of the subtitle, and proper nouns; all other words begin with small letters. In titles of journals, capitalize all significant words. Unless your instructor specifies italics, underline the titles of books and journals, along with any comma or period following. Do not underline or use quotation marks around the titles of articles.

City of publication

For sources that are not periodicals (such as books or government publications), give the city of publication. The following US cities do not require state names as well: Baltimore, Boston, Chicago, Los Angeles, New York, Philadelphia, and San Francisco.

Follow their names with a colon. For all other cities, add a comma after the city name and give the two-letter postal abbreviation of the state (see p. 80). Then put a colon after the state.

Publisher's name

Also for nonperiodical sources, give the publisher's name after the place of publication and a colon. Use shortened names for many publishers (such as "Morrow" for William Morrow), and omit "Co.," "Inc.," and "Publishers." However, give full names for associations, corporations, and university presses (such as "Harvard University Press"), and do not omit "Books" or "Press" from a publisher's name.

Page numbers

Use the abbreviation "p." or "pp." before page numbers in books and in newspapers, but *not* in other periodicals. For inclusive page numbers, include all figures: "667–668."

Note If the following pages don't provide a model for a kind of source you used, try to find one that comes close, and provide ample information so that readers can trace the source. Often, you will have to combine models to cite a source accurately—for instance, combining "A book with two or more authors" (2) and "An article in a journal" (11) for a journal article with two or more authors.

Books

1. A book with one author

Rodriguez, R. (1982). A hunger of memory: The education of Richard Rodriguez. Boston: Godine.

The initial "R" appears instead of the author's first name, even though the author's full first name appears on the source. In the title, only the first words of title and subtitle and the proper name are capitalized.

2. A book with two or more authors

Nesselroade, J. R., & Baltes, P. B. (1999). Longitudinal research in behavioral studies. New York: Academic Press.

An ampersand (&) separates the authors' names.

3. A book with an editor

Dohrenwend, B. S., & Dohrenwend, B. P. (Eds.). (1994). Stressful life events: Their nature and effects. New York: Wiley.

List the editors' names as if they were authors, but follow the last name with "(Eds.)."—or "(Ed.)." with only one editor. Note the periods inside and outside the final parenthesis.

APA References

4. A book with a translator

Trajan, P. D. (1927). Psychology of animals (H. Simone, Trans.). Washington, DC: Halperin.

The name of the translator appears in parentheses after the title, followed by a comma, "Trans.," a closing parenthesis, and a final period. Note also the absence of periods in "DC."

5. A book with a group author

Lorenz Research. (1997). Research in social studies teaching. Baltimore: Arrow Books.

For a work with a group author—such as a research group, government agency, or corporation—begin the entry with the group name.

In the references list, alphabetize the work as if the first main word (excluding *The, A,* and *An*) were an author's last name.

6. An anonymous book

Merriam-Webster's collegiate dictionary (10th ed.). (1997). Springfield, MA: Merriam-Webster.

When no author is named, list the work under its title, and alphabetize it by the first main word (excluding *The, A, An*).

7. Two or more works by the same author(s) published in the same year

Gardner, H. (1973a). The arts and human development. New York: Wiley.

Gardner, H. (1973b). The quest for mind: Piaget, Lévi-Strauss, and the structuralist movement. New York: Knopf.

When citing two or more works by exactly the same author(s), published in the same year—as in the examples above—arrange them alphabetically by the first main word of the title and distinguish the sources by adding a letter to the date. Both the date *and* the letter are used in citing the source in your text (see p. 49).

When citing two or more works by exactly the same author(s) but *not* published in the same year, arrange the sources in order of their publication dates, earliest first.

8. A later edition

Bollinger, D. L. (1975). Aspects of language (2nd ed.). New York: Harcourt Brace Jovanovich.

The edition number in parentheses follows the title and is followed by a period.

9. A work in more than one volume

Lincoln, A. (1953). The collected works of Abraham Lincoln (R. P. Basler, Ed.). (Vol. 5). New Brunswick, NJ: Rutgers University Press.

Lincoln, A. (1953). The collected works of Abraham Lincoln (R. P. Basler, Ed.). (Vols. 1-8). New Brunswick, NJ: Rutgers University Press.

The first entry cites a single volume (5) in the eight-volume set. The second cites all eight volumes. Use the abbreviation "Vol." or "Vols." in parentheses, and follow the closing parenthesis with a period. In the absence of an editor's name, the description of volumes would follow the title directly: The collected works of Abraham Lincoln (Vol. 5).

10. An article or chapter in an edited book

Paykel, E. S. (1994). Life stress and psychiatric disorder: Applications of the clinical approach. In B. S. Dohrenwend & B. P. Dohrenwend (Eds.), Stressful life events: Their nature and effects (pp. 239-264). New York: Wiley.

Give the publication date of the collection (1994 above) as the publication date of the article or chapter. After the article or chapter title and a period, say "In" and then provide the editors' names (in normal order), "(Eds.)" and a comma, the title of the collection, and the page numbers of the article in parentheses.

Periodicals: Journals, magazines, newspapers

11. An article in a journal with continuous pagination throughout the annual volume

Emery, R. E. (1992). Marital turmoil: Interpersonal conflict and the children of discord and divorce. Psychological Bulletin, 92, 310-330.

See page 22 for an explanation of journal pagination. Note that you do not place the article title in quotation marks and that you capitalize only the first words of the title and subtitle. In contrast, you underline the journal title and capitalize all significant words. Separate the volume number from the title with a comma, and underline the number. Do not add "pp." before the page numbers.

12. An article in a journal that pages issues separately

Dacey, J. (1998). Management participation in corporate buy-outs. Management Perspectives, 7(4), 20-31.

Consult page 22 for an explanation of journal pagination. In this case, place the issue number in parentheses after the volume number without intervening space. Do *not* underline the issue number.

13. An abstract of a journal article

Emery, R. E. (1992). Marital turmoil: Interpersonal conflict and the children of discord and divorce. Psychological Bulletin, 92, 310-330. (From Psychological Abstracts, 69, Item 1320)

When you cite the abstract of an article, rather than the article itself, give full publication information for the article, followed, in parentheses, by the information for the collection of abstracts, including title, volume number, and either page number or other reference number ("Item 1320" above). If it is not otherwise clear that you are citing an abstract (because the word *abstract* does not appear in the title of the periodical or of the abstracts collection), add "[Abstract]" between the source title and the following period. See model 19 on the next page for an example.

14. An article in a magazine

Van Gelder, L. (1996, December). Countdown to motherhood: When should you have a baby? Ms., 37-39, 74.

If a magazine has volume and issue numbers, give them as in models 11 and 12. Also give the full date of the issue: year, followed by a comma, month, and day (if any). Give all page numbers even when the article appears on discontinuous pages, without "pp."

15. An article in a newspaper

Lewis, P. H. (1999, January 21). Many updates cause profitable confusion. The New York Times, pp. D1, D5.

Give month *and* day along with year of publication. Use The in the newspaper name if the paper itself does. For a newspaper (unlike a journal or magazine), precede the page number(s) with "p." or "pp."

16. An unsigned article

The right to die. (1976, October 11). Time, 121, 101.

List and alphabetize the article under its title, as you would an anonymous book (model 6, p. 54).

17. A review

Dinnage, R. (1987, November 29). Against the master and his men [Review of the book A mind of her own: The life of Karen Horney]. The New York Times Book Review, 10-11.

If the review is not titled, use the bracketed information as the title, keeping the brackets.

Electronic sources

The APA *Publication Manual* includes a few models for electronic sources. More recently, the APA Web site (see p. 46) has added new models that extend and in some ways alter those in the *Publication Manual.* The following examples reflect the more recent guidelines when appropriate.

In general, the APA's electronic-source references begin as those for print references do: author(s), date, title. Then you add information on when and how you retrieved the source—for example, Retrieved January 8, 1999 from the World Wide Web: http://www.liasu.edu/finance-dl/46732 (in APA style, no period follows an electronic address at the end of the reference).

Two sources provide more models for electronic sources based on APA style. Each one also differs from APA style, however, so ask your instructor which style you should use.

- Columbia online style for the sciences is discussed in this book's Chapter 6. The differences between APA and Columbia are outlined on page 75.
- Xia Li and Nancy B. Crane's *Electronic Style: A Guide to Citing Electronic Information* (1993) was a source for the APA *Publication Manual.* Li and Crane's formats have since been updated at *http://www.uvm.edu/%7encrane/estyles/apa.html.*

Note Since APA sources do not specify how to break electronic addresses in references, follow MLA style: break only after slashes, and do not hyphenate.

18. A periodical article on CD-ROM

Emery, R. E. (1992). Marital turmoil: Interpersonal conflict and the children of discord and divorce. Psychological Bulletin, 92, 310-330. Retrieved from ERIC database (ERIC Document Reproduction Service, CD-ROM, No. EJ 426 821)

19. An abstract on CD-ROM

Willard, B. L. (1992). Changes in occupational safety standards, 1970-1990 [Abstract]. Retrieved from UMI-ProQuest (Dissertation Abstracts, CD-ROM, Item 7770763)

20. An article in an online journal

Palfrey, A. (1996). Choice of mates in identical twins. Modern Psychology, 4(1). Retrieved February 25, 2000 from the World Wide Web: http://www.liasu.edu/modpsy/palfrey4(1).htm

21. An article in an online newspaper

Still, L. (1996, March 3). On the battlefields of business, millions of casualties. The New York Times on the Web. Retrieved August 17, 1999 from the World Wide Web: http://www.nytimes.com/specials/downsize/03downl.htm

22. A retrievable online posting

Tourville, M. (1999, January 6). European currency reform. International Finance Discussion List. Retrieved January 8, 1999 from the World Wide Web: http://www.liasu.edu/finance-dl/46732

Include postings to discussion lists and newsgroups in your list of references only if they are retrievable by others. The source above is archived and thus retrievable.

23. A nonretrievable online posting

At least one member of the research team has expressed reservations about the design of the study (L. Kogod, personal communication, February 6, 2000).

Personal electronic mail and other online postings that are not retrievable by others should be cited only in your text, as in the example above. If the author's name is given in the text, omit it from the citation: (personal communication, February 6, 2000).

24. A source from an online database

Wilkins, J. M. (1999, December 12). The myths of the only child. Psychology Update, 16-20. Retrieved December 20, 1999 from ProQuest Direct database (ProQuest Health and Medical Complete) on the World Wide Web: http://www.umi.com/proquest/

The retrieval statement includes the online service (here, ProQuest Direct database); the name of the particular database on which you found your source, in parentheses; and the address of the service's home page.

25. Software

Project scheduler 8000 [Computer software]. (1999). Orlando, FL: Scitor.

Other sources

26. A report

Gerald, K. (1958). Medico-moral problems in obstetric care (Report No. NP-71). St. Louis, MO: Catholic Hospital Association.

Treat the report like a book, but provide any report number in parentheses immediately after the title, with no punctuation between them.

For a report from the Educational Resources Information Center (ERIC), provide the ERIC document number in parentheses at the end of the entry:

Jolson, M. K. (1981). Music education for preschoolers (Report No. TC-622). New York: Teachers College, Columbia University. (ERIC Document Reproduction Service No. ED 264 488)

27. A government publication

U.S. House. Committee on Ways and Means. (1991). Medicare payment for outpatient physical and occupational therapy services. 102d Cong., 2d Sess. Washington, DC: U.S. Government Printing Office.

Stiller, A. (1996). Historic preservation and tax incentives. U.S. Department of the Interior. Washington, DC: U.S. Government Printing Office.

Hawaii. Department of Education. (1998). Kauai district schools, profile 1998-99. Honolulu, HI: Author.

If no individual is given as the author, list the publication under the name of the sponsoring agency. When the agency is both the author and the publisher, use "Author" in place of the publisher's name.

28. An abstract of an unpublished dissertation

Steciw, S. K. (1986). Alterations to the Pessac project of Le Corbusier (Doctoral dissertation, University of Cambridge, England, 1986). Dissertation Abstracts International, 46, 565C.

For an abstract of an unpublished doctoral dissertation, give the university and the year of the dissertation in parentheses after the title. Then give the source of the abstract, the volume number, and the page number.

29. An interview

Brisick, W. C. (1988, July 1). [Interview with Ishmael Reed]. Publishers Weekly, 41-42.

List a published interview under the interviewer's name. Provide the publication information for the kind of source the interview appears in (here, a magazine). Immediately after the date, in brackets, specify that the piece is an interview and give the subject's name if necessary. For an interview with a title, follow model 17 (p. 56).

Note that interviews you conduct yourself are not included in the list of references. Instead, use an in-text parenthetical citation, as shown in model 23 (p. 58) for a nonretrievable online posting.

30. A videotape, recording, or other audiovisual source

Spielberg, S. (Director). (1993). Schindler's list [Videotape]. Los Angeles: Viacom.

Siberry, J. (1995). Caravan. On Maria [CD]. Burbank, CA: Reprise.

For audiovisual sources such as films, videotapes, television or radio programs, or recordings, begin with the name of the person whose work you are citing, followed by his or her function, if appropriate, in parentheses. Immediately after the title, give the medium in brackets. Then give the location and name of the distributor.

CHAPTER 5

CBE Style

5a Citing sources in the sciences: CBE style

Within the natural and applied sciences, the practitioners of each discipline use a slightly different style of documentation and manuscript format. Following are some of the style guides most often consulted:

American Chemical Society. *ACS Style Guide: A Manual for Authors and Editors.* 2nd ed. 1997.
American Institute of Physics. *Style Manual for Guidance in the Preparation of Papers.* 4th ed. 1990.
American Mathematical Society. *A Manual for Authors of Mathematical Papers.* Rev. ed. 1990.
American Medical Association. *Manual of Style.* 8th ed. 1989.
Bates, Robert L., Rex Buchanan, and Marla Adkins-Heljeson, eds. *Geowriting: A Guide to Writing, Editing, and Printing in Earth Science.* 5th ed. 1992.
Council of Biology Editors. *Scientific Style and Format: The CBE Manual for Authors, Editors, and Publishers.* 6th ed. 1994.

Writers in the life sciences, physical sciences, and sometimes mathematics rely for documentation style on *Scientific Style and Format* from the Council of Biology Editors (CBE). This book details the two styles of in-text citation discussed here: one using author and date and one using numbers. Both types of text citation refer to a list of references at the end of the paper (see opposite). Ask your instructor which style you should use.

1 Using CBE name-year text citations

In the CBE name-year style, parenthetical text citations provide the last name of the author being cited and the source's year of pub-

http://www.wisc.edu/writing/Handbook/DocCBE6.html Guidance on CBE documentation style, from the University of Wisconsin at Madison.

lication. At the end of the paper, a list of references, arranged alphabetically by authors' last names, provides complete information on each source. (See opposite.)

The CBE name-year style closely resembles the APA name-year style detailed on pages 46–50. You can follow the APA examples for in-text citations, making several notable changes for CBE:

- Do not use a comma to separate the author's name and the date: (Baumrind 1968, p. 34).
- For sources with two authors, separate their names with "and" (not "&"): (Pepinsky and DeStefano 1987).
- For sources with three or more authors, use "and others" (not "et al.") after the first author's name: (Rutter and others 1996).
- For anonymous sources, give the author as "Anonymous" both in the citation and in the list of references: (Anonymous 1976).

2 Using CBE numbered text citations

In the CBE number style, raised numbers in the text refer to a numbered list of references at the end of the paper.

> Two standard references[1,2] use this term.
>
> These forms of immunity have been extensively researched.[3]
>
> According to one report,[4] research into some forms of viral immunity is almost nonexistent.
>
> Hepburn and Tatin[2] do not discuss this project.

Assignment of numbers

The number for each source is based on the order in which you cite the source in the text: the first cited source is 1, the second is 2, and so on.

Reuse of numbers

When you cite a source you have already cited and numbered, use the original number again (see the last example above, which reuses the number 2 from the first example).

This reuse is the key difference between the CBE numbered citations and numbered references to footnotes or endnotes (pp. 37–45). In the CBE style, each source has only one number, determined by the order in which the source is cited. With notes, in contrast, the numbering proceeds in sequence, so that sources have as many numbers as they have citations in the text.

Citation of two or more sources

When you cite two or more sources at once, arrange their numbers in sequence and separate them with a comma and no space, as in the first example on the previous page.

3 Using a CBE reference list

For both the name-year and the number styles of in-text citation, provide a list, titled "References," of all sources you have cited. Format the page as shown for APA references on page 50 (but you may omit the shortened title before the page number).

Follow these guidelines for references, noting the important differences in name-year and number styles:

Spacing

Single-space each entry, and double-space between entries.

Arrangement

The two styles differ in their arrangement of entries:

Name-year style:

Arrange entries alphabetically by authors' last names.

Number style:

Arrange entries in numerical order—that is, in order of their citation in the text.

Format

In both styles, begin the first line of each entry at the left margin and indent subsequent lines:

Name-year style:

Hepburn PX, Tatin JM. 1995. Human physiology. New York: Columbia Univ Pr. 1026 p.

Number style:

2. Hepburn PX, Tatin JM. Human physiology. New York: Columbia Univ Pr; 1995. 1026 p.

Authors

List each author's name with the last name first, followed by initials for first and middle names. (See the examples above.) Do not use a comma after the last name or periods or space with the initials. Do use a comma to separate authors' names.

CBE References

Placement of dates

The two styles differ, as shown in the examples on the facing page.

Name-year style:

The date follows the author's or authors' names.

Number Style:

The date follows the publication information (for a book) or the title (for a periodical).

Journal titles

Do not underline or italicize journal titles. For titles of two or more words, abbreviate words of six or more letters (without periods) and omit most prepositions, articles, and conjunctions. Capitalize each word. For example, *Annals of Medicine* becomes Ann Med, and *Journal of Chemical and Biochemical Studies* becomes J Chem Biochem Stud. See the Rowell examples on the facing page.

Book and article titles

Do not underline, italicize, or quote a book or an article title. Capitalize only the first word and any proper nouns. See the Rowell and Hepburn and Tatin examples on the facing page.

Publication information for journal articles

Both the name-year and the number styles give the journal's volume number, a colon, and the inclusive page numbers of the article: 28:329-33 in the examples below. (If the journal has an issue number, it follows the volume number in parentheses: 62(2):26-40.) However, the styles differ in the punctuation as well as the placement of the date:

Name-year style:

The date, after the author's name and a period, is followed by a period:

> Rowell LB. 1996. Blood pressure regulation during exercise. Ann Med 28:329-33.

Number style:

The date, after the journal title and a space, is followed by a semicolon:

> 3. Rowell LB. Blood pressure regulation during exercise. Ann Med 1996;28:329-33.

The following examples show both a name-year reference and a number reference for each type of source.

Books

1. A book with one author

Gould SJ. 1987. Time's arrow, time's cycle. Cambridge: Harvard Univ Pr. 222 p.

1. Gould SJ. Time's arrow, time's cycle. Cambridge: Harvard Univ Pr; 1987. 222 p.

2. A book with two to ten authors

Hepburn PX, Tatin JM. 1995. Human physiology. New York: Columbia Univ Pr. 1026 p.

2. Hepburn PX, Tatin JM. Human physiology. New York: Columbia Univ Pr; 1995. 1026 p.

3. A book with more than ten authors

Evans RW, Bowditch L, Dana KL, Drummond A, Wildovitch WP, Young SL, Mills P, Mills RR, Livak SR, Lisi OL, and others. 1998. Organ transplants: ethical issues. Ann Arbor: Univ of Michigan Pr. 498 p.

3. Evans RW, Bowditch L, Dana KL, Drummond A, Wildovitch WP, Young SL, Mills P, Mills RR, Livak SR, Lisi OL, and others. Organ transplants: ethical issues. Ann Arbor: Univ of Michigan Pr; 1998. 498 p.

4. A book with an editor

Jonson P, editor. 1997. Anatomy yearbook. Los Angeles: Anatco. 628 p.

4. Jonson P, editor. Anatomy yearbook. Los Angeles: Anatco; 1997. 628 p.

5. A selection from a book

Krigel R, Laubenstein L, Muggia F. 1997. Kaposi's sarcoma. In: Ebbeson P, Biggar RS, Melbye M, editors. AIDS: a basic guide for clinicians. 2nd ed. Philadelphia: WB Saunders. p 100-26.

5. Krigel R, Laubenstein L, Muggia F. Kaposi's sarcoma. In: Ebbeson P, Biggar RS, Melbye M, editors. AIDS: a basic guide for clinicians. 2nd ed. Philadelphia: WB Saunders; 1997. p 100-26.

6. An anonymous work

[Anonymous]. 1992. Health care for multiple sclerosis. New York: US Health Care. 86 p.

6. [Anonymous]. Health care for multiple sclerosis. New York: US Health Care; 1992. 86 p.

7. Two or more cited works by the same author published in the same year

Gardner H. 1973a. The arts and human development. New York: J Wiley. 406 p.

Gardner H. 1973b. The quest for mind: Piaget, Lévi-Strauss, and the structuralist movement. New York: AA Knopf. 492 p.

(The number style does not require such forms.)

Periodicals: Journals, magazines, newspapers

8. An article in a journal with continuous pagination throughout the annual volume

Ancino R, Carter KV, Elwin DJ. 1983. Factors contributing to viral immunity: a review of the research. Dev Biol 30:156-9.

8. Ancino R, Carter KV, Elwin DJ. Factors contributing to viral immunity: a review of the research. Dev Biol 1983;30:156-9.

9. An article in a journal that pages issues separately

Kim P. 1986 Feb. Medical decision making for the dying. Milbank Quar 64(2):26-40.

9. Kim P. Medical decision making for the dying. Milbank Quar 1986 Feb;64(2):26-40.

10. An article in a newspaper

Krauthammer C. 1986 June 13. Lifeboat ethics: the case of Baby Jesse. Washington Post;Sect A:33(col 1).

10. Krauthammer C. Lifeboat ethics: the case of Baby Jesse. Washington Post 1986 June 13;Sect A:33(col 1).

11. An article in a magazine

Van Gelder L. 1986 Dec. Countdown to motherhood: when should you have a baby? Ms.:37-9.

11. Van Gelder L. Countdown to motherhood: when should you have a baby? Ms. 1986 Dec:37-9.

Electronic sources

The CBE's *Scientific Style and Format* includes just a few models for electronic sources, and they form the basis of the following examples. For additional models and simpler formats, you can use Columbia online style for the sciences, discussed in Chapter 6. Pages 75–76 show how to adapt Columbia style to the CBE styles (both name-year and number) and detail the differences between the styles. Ask your instructor which style you should use.

Note Since the CBE does not specify how to break electronic addresses, follow MLA style: break only after slashes, and do not hyphenate.

12. A source on CD-ROM

Reich WT, editor. 1998. Encyclopedia of bioethics [CD-ROM]. New York: Co-Health.

12. Reich WT, editor. Encyclopedia of bioethics [CD-ROM]. New York: Co-Health; 1998.

13. An online journal article

Grady GF. 1993 May 2. The here and now of hepatitis B immunization. Today's Med [serial online]. Available from: http://www.fmrt.org/todaysmedicine/Grady050293.html. Accessed 1999 Dec 27.

13. Grady GF. The here and now of hepatitis B immunization. Today's Med [serial online] 1993 May 2. Available from: http://www.fmrt.org/todaysmedicine/Grady050293.html. Accessed 1999 Dec 27.

14. An online book

Ruch BJ, Ruch DB. 1999. Homeopathy and medicine: resolving the conflict [book online]. New York: Albert Einstein Coll of Medicine. Available from: http://www.einstein.edu/medicine/books/ruch.html. Accessed 2000 Jan 28.

14. Ruch BJ, Ruch DB. Homeopathy and medicine: resolving the conflict [book online]. New York: Albert Einstein Coll of Medicine; 1999. Available from: http://www.einstein.edu/medicine/books/ruch.html. Accessed 2000 Jan 28.

15. Computer software

Project scheduler 8000 [computer program]. 1999. Version 4.1. Orlando (FL): Scitor. 1 computer disk: 3 1/2 in. Accompanied by: 1 manual. System requirements: IBM PC or fully compatible computer; DOS 6.0 or higher; Windows 3.1 or higher; 8 MB RAM; hard disk with a minimum of 2 MB of free space.

15. Project scheduler 8000 [computer program]. Version 4.1. Orlando (FL): Scitor; 1999. 1 computer disk: 3 1/2 in. Accompanied by: 1 manual. System requirements: IBM PC or fully compatible computer; DOS 6.0 or higher; Windows 3.1 or higher; 8 MB RAM; hard disk with a minimum of 2 MB of free space.

Other sources

16. A government publication

Committee on Science and Technology, House (US). 1991. Hearing on procurement and allocation of human organs for transplantation. 102nd Cong., 1st Sess. House Doc. nr 409.

16. Committee on Science and Technology, House (US). Hearing on procurement and allocation of human organs for transplantation. 102nd Cong., 1st Sess. House Doc. nr 409; 1991.

17. A nongovernment report

Warnock M. 1992. Report of the Committee on Fertilization and Embryology. Baylor University, Department of Embryology. Waco (TX): Baylor Univ. Report nr BU/DE.4261.

17. Warnock M. Report of the Committee on Fertilization and Embryology. Baylor University, Department of Embryology. Waco (TX): Baylor Univ; 1992. Report nr BU/DE.4261.

18. A sound recording, video recording, or film

Teaching Media. 1993. Cell mitosis [videocassette]. White Plains (NY): Teaching Media. 1 videocassette: 40 min, sound, black and white, 1/2 in.

18. Cell mitosis [videocassette]. White Plains (NY): Teaching Media; 1993. 1 videocassette: 40 min, sound, black and white, 1/2 in.

CHAPTER 6

Columbia Style for Online Sources

The style manuals in many disciplines do not yet provide detailed guidelines for citing the many kinds of sources available on the Internet. In response, Janice R. Walker and Todd Taylor wrote *The Columbia Guide to Online Style,* published by Columbia University Press in 1998.

The Columbia Guide offers models for both the humanities and the sciences. The humanities models reflect MLA style (Chapter 2), and the science models reflect APA style (Chapter 4)—although there are differences in both cases. The Columbia models can also be adapted for the other two styles covered in this book: Chicago for the humanities (Chapter 3) and CBE for the sciences (Chapter 5).

6a Distinguishing the elements of Columbia style

Columbia style adapts MLA and APA styles, but it also stresses the likely and important elements that allow readers to trace online sources. These elements may be the same as those in conventional printed sources, but often they are not.

Author

The author may be identified only by a login name (such as *jqsmith*) or a fictitious name (such as *c_major*). List the source by this name if it's all you can find, but take special care in evaluating and using such a source. Cite a source with no identifiable author by its title.

Title

For the title of a complete work, such as a book or periodical, use italics rather than underlining. If your document were posted on the Web, underlining would signal a hypertext link. Also italicize the titles of online sites and the names of information services.

http://www.columbia.edu/cu/cup/cgos An overview of Columbia online style, with updates, from Columbia University Press.

Date of access

Online sources may change often, so always provide the date of your access so that readers know which version you used. The date falls at the end of the citation, in parentheses, and in the format "day mo. year"—for instance, (31 Aug. 1998). If the source's publication or revision date and your access date are identical, use only the access date.

Electronic address

Always provide an online source's exact and complete electronic address—the complete path for readers to follow in retrieving the source themselves. The address falls just before the access date with no special introduction or additional punctuation—for instance, finance-dl@weg.isu.edu (31 Aug. 1998). Follow MLA style for breaking long addresses: break only after slashes, and do not hyphenate.

6b Citing online sources in the humanities

Columbia online style adapts most elements of MLA documentation (Chapter 2) to provide a thorough system for documenting online sources in the humanities.

- As in MLA style, a citation in the text provides the author's last name and the page or other number where the borrowed material appears—for instance, One researcher disagrees (Johnson 143) or Johnson disagrees (143). (See pp. 5–11 for a variety of examples.) Because many online sources do not use page, paragraph, section, or other numbers, in-text citations of electronic sources may consist only of the author's name.
- Also as in MLA style, a list titled "Works Cited" at the end of your paper arranges your sources alphabetically by the author's last name, or by the first main word of the title if there is no author.

Key differences from MLA style

Columbia online style differs from MLA style (pp. 24–32) in several ways:

Columbia online style	MLA style
Titles of complete works (books, journals) are italicized.	Titles of complete works are underlined.
The electronic address precedes the date of your access and is not enclosed in angle brackets: finance-dl@weg.isu.edu (23 Feb. 1997).	The electronic address follows the date of your access and is enclosed in angle brackets: 23 Feb. 1997 <finance-dl@weg.isu.edu>.

Columbia online style	MLA style
The date of access is enclosed in parentheses.	The date of access is not enclosed in parentheses.
The publication medium is not specially identified.	The publication medium—for instance, "Online posting"—sometimes appears after the title.

Ask your instructor which format you should use for online sources.

Chicago style

You can merge Columbia humanities style and Chicago humanities style (Chapter 3) to create citations for online sources that Chicago does not currently cover. The following note and works-cited models show such mergers, drawing on Chicago examples given on page 43.

Footnote or endnote

15. Jane Austen, *Emma,* ed. Ronald Blythe (Harmondsworth, Eng.: Penguin, 1972). *Oxford Text Archive.* ftp://ota.ox.ac.uk/public/english/Austen/emma.1519 (15 Dec. 1999).

Works-cited entry

Austen, Jane. *Emma.* Edited by Ronald Blythe. Harmondsworth, Eng.: Penguin, 1972. *Oxford Text Archive.* ftp://ota.ox.ac.uk/public/english/Austen/emma.1519 (15 Dec. 1999).

These Columbia-Chicago mergers differ from the corresponding Chicago models in several ways:

Columbia online style	Chicago style
The publication medium is not specially identified.	The publication medium—for instance, "book online"—appears after the title in brackets.
The electronic address precedes the date of your access at the end of the entry, and neither is introduced. See the works-cited entry above.	The positions of the electronic address and the access date vary, and both are introduced. In the Chicago works-cited entry for the Austen book, the access date follows the publication date of 1972—Accessed 15 December 1999—and the address falls at the end of the entry—Available from ftp://ota.ox.ac.uk/public/english/Austen/emma.1519; Internet.
The date of access is enclosed in parentheses, and the month is abbreviated.	The date of access is not enclosed in parentheses, and the month is spelled out.

Columbia works-cited models for the humanities

Ask your instructor which format you should use for online sources.

Models of Columbia humanities style

1. A site on the World Wide Web

Lederman, Leon. *Topics in Modern Physics--Lederman.* 10 Oct. 1999. http://www-ed.fnal.gov/samplers/hsphys/people/lederman.html (12 Dec. 1999).

2. A revised or modified site

Ruggira, Wendy. "Chiropractic: Past, Present and Future." *Chiromen.com.* Mod. 30 Sept. 1999. http://chiromen.com/chiropractic.htm (4 Feb. 2000).

3. A book

A book previously published in print:

James, Henry. *The Turn of the Screw.* New York: Scribner's, 1908-09. 1998. *American Literary Classics a Chapter a Day.* http://www.americanliterature.com/TS/TSINDX.HTML (4 Mar. 2000).

An original book:

Cooper, Phoebe, ed. *Sam and Daphne Maeglin: Selected Correspondence, 1940-1964.* 1999. http://www.alphabetica.org/maeglin (21 Mar. 2000).

4. An article in a periodical

Palfrey, Andrew. "Choice of Mates in Identical Twins." *Modern Psychology* 4.1 (1996): 12 pars. http://www.liasu.edu/modpsy/palfrey4(1).htm (25 Feb. 2000).

5. A group or organization as author

Exxon Corporation. "Managing Risk." *Environment, Health and Safety Progress Report.* 1999. http://www.exxon.com/exxoncorp/news/safety_report/index.html (6 Apr. 2000).

United States. Dept. of State. Bureau of Public Affairs. *History of the National Security Council, 1947-1997.* Aug. 1998. http://www.whitehouse.gov/WH/EOP/NSC/html/History.html (6 Feb. 1999).

6. A maintained or compiled site

Scots Teaching and Research Network. Maint. John Corbett. 2 Feb. 1998. U of Glasgow. http://www.arts.gla.ac.uk/www/comet/starn.htm (5 Mar. 2000).

7. A graphic, video, or audio file

Hamilton, Calvin J. "Components of Comets." 1997. *Space Art.* wysisiwyg://94/http://spaceart.com/solar/eng/comet.htm (20 Dec. 1999).

8. Personal electronic mail

Millon, Michele. "Re: Grief Therapy." Personal e-mail (4 May 1999).

9. A posting to a discussion list

Tourville, Michael. "European Currency Reform." 6 Jan. 1999. *International Finance Discussion List.* finance-dl@weg.isu.edu (8 Jan. 1999).

10. A posting to a newsgroup or forum

Cramer, Sherry. "Recent Investment Practices." 26 Mar. 2000. news:biz.investment.current.2700 (3 Apr. 2000).

11. An archived posting

Tourville, Michael. "European Currency Reform." 6 Jan. 1999. *International Finance Discussion List.* http://www.weg.isu.edu/finance-dl/46732 (2 June 1999).

12. An encyclopedia

White, Geoffrey. "Ethnopsychology." *The MIT Encyclopedia of Cognitive Sciences.* Ed. Rob Wilson and Frank Keil. Cambridge: MIT P, 1997. http://mitpress.mit.edu/MITECS/work/whiteg_r.html (26 Mar. 1999).

13. A database

United States. Dept. of Health and Human Services. "Depression Is a Treatable Illness: A Patient's Guide." Apr. 1993. *Health Services Technology Assessment Texts.* No. 93-0533. http://text.nlm.nih.gov/ftrs/pick?collect=930533 (26 Sept. 1999).

14. A gopher or FTP site

Provide directions to a specific source in one of two ways: give the unique address of the file, as in the example above; or give the address of the home page, a space, and the path to the file, as in this example:

Goetsch, Sallie. "And What About Costume?" *Didaskalia: Ancient Theatre Today* 2.2 (1995). gopher://gopher.warwicku.ac.uk Didaskalia/Didaskalia: Ancient Theatre Today/1995/03Features/Goetsch (26 May 1999).

15. A telnet site

Johnson, Earl. "My House: Come In." *Houses of Cyberspace.* 7 Aug. 1999. telnet://edwin.ohms.bookso.com.7777 @go #50827, press 10 (11 Aug. 1999).

16. A synchronous communication

Wendy_Librarian_. "Online Integrity (#421)." *Internet Public Library MOO.* telnet://moo.ipl.org.8888 @go #421 (4 Jan. 1999).

17. Software

Project Scheduler 8000. Vers. 4.1. Orlando: Scitor, 1999.

6c Citing online sources in the sciences

Columbia style adapts most elements of APA style (Chapter 4) to provide a thorough system for documenting online sources in the social, natural, and applied sciences.

- As in APA style, a citation in the text provides the author's last name, the date of publication, and the page or other number where specific borrowings appear—for instance, One researcher called the study "deeply flawed" (Johnson, 1998, p. 143) or Johnson (1998) called the study "deeply flawed" (p. 143). (See pp. 46–50 for a variety of examples.) Because many online sources do not use page, paragraph, or other numbers, citations of specific borrowings from electronic sources often consist only of the author's name and the date.
- Also as in APA style, a list titled "References" at the end of your paper arranges your sources alphabetically by the author's last name, or by the first main word of the title if there is no author.

Key differences from APA style

Though it includes many more kinds of online sources than APA style currently does, Columbia style does differ from APA style (pp. 56–58) in several significant ways:

Columbia online style	APA style
Titles of complete works (books, journals) are italicized.	Titles of complete works are underlined.
A full publication date after the author's name is in the format "year, month day": 1999, December 12. All other dates are in the format "day mo. year": 12 Dec. 1999.	A full publication date after the author's name is in the format "year, month day": 1999, December 12. All other dates are in the format "month day, year": December 12, 1999.
The electronic address precedes the date of your access, with the date in parentheses—for instance, http://www.thinck.com/insec.html (21 Jan. 1998).	The electronic address follows the date of your access, and the two are linked in a statement—for instance, Retrieved January 21, 1998 from the World Wide Web: http://www.thinck.com/insec.html
A period ends the entry.	A period does not end the entry.

Ask your instructor which format you should use for online sources.

CBE style

CBE style (Chapter 5) currently provides few models for citing online sources. By merging Columbia science style and either the CBE name-year style or the CBE number style, you can create citations for kinds of sources not covered by CBE, such as the Web site following.

Columbia reference models for the sciences

Name-year style

Lederman L. 1997 Oct 10. *Topics in modern physics--Lederman.* http://www-ed.fnal.gov/samplers/hsphys/people/lederman.html (12 Dec. 1999).

Number style

4. Lederman L. *Topics in modern physics--Lederman.* 1997 Oct 10. http://www-ed.fnal.gov/samplers/hsphys/people/lederman.html (12 Dec. 1999).

Such mergers of Columbia and CBE styles involve some alterations in the CBE models shown on pages 67–68.

Columbia online style	CBE style
The publication medium is not specially identified.	The publication medium—for instance, "serial online"—appears in brackets after the title.
The electronic address and the date of your access are not introduced—for instance, finance-dl@weg.isu.edu (23 Feb. 1997).	Both the electronic address and the date of your access are introduced—for instance, Available from: finance-dl@weg.isu.edu. Accessed 1997 Feb 23.
The date of access is enclosed in parentheses and is in the format "day mo. year" (the month abbreviated with a period).	The date of access is not enclosed in parentheses and is in the format "year mo day" (the month abbreviated without a period).

Ask your instructor which format you should use for online sources.

Models of Columbia science style

1. A site on the World Wide Web

Lederman, L. (1999, October 10). *Topics in modern physics--Lederman.* http://www-ed.fnal.gov/samplers/hsphys/people/lederman.html (12 Dec. 1999).

2. A revised or modified site

Ruggira, W. (1998). Chiropractic: Past, present and future (Mod. 30 Sept. 1999). *Chiromen.com.* http://chiromen.com/chiropractic.htm (4 Feb. 2000).

3. A book

A book previously published in print:

James, H. (1998). *The turn of the screw.* New York: Scribner's, 1908-1909. *American literary classics a chapter a day.* http://www.americanliterature.com/TS/TSINDX.HTML (4 Mar. 2000).

An original book:

Cooper, P. (Ed.). (1999). *Sam and Daphne Maeglin: Selected correspondence, 1940-1964.* http://www.alphabetica.org/maeglin (21 Mar. 2000).

4. An article in a periodical

Palfrey, A. (1996). Choice of mates in identical twins. *Modern Psychology, 4*(1). http://www.liasu.edu/modpsy/palfrey4(1).htm (25 Feb. 1999).

5. A group or organization as author

Exxon Corporation. (1999). Managing risk. *Environment, health and safety progress report.* http://www.exxon.com/exxoncorp/news/publications/safety_report/index.html (6 Apr. 2000).

U.S. Department of State. Bureau of Public Affairs. (1998, August). *History of the National Security Council, 1947-1997.* http://www.whitehouse.gov/WH/EOP/NSC/html/History.html (6 Feb. 1999).

6. A maintained or compiled site

Scots teaching and research network. (1998, February 2). (J. Corbett, Maint.). University of Glasgow. http://www.arts.gla.ac.uk/www/comet/starn.html (5 Mar. 2000).

7. A graphic, video, or audio file

Hamilton, C. J. (1997). Components of comets [graphic file]. *Space art.* wysisiwyg://94/http://spaceart.com/solar/eng/comet.htm (20 Dec. 1999).

8. Personal electronic mail

Millon, M. Re: Grief therapy [personal e-mail]. (4 May 1999).

Note that APA style calls for citing nonretrievable sources only in your text (see p. 58).

9. A posting to a discussion list

Tourville, M. (1999, January 6). European currency reform. *International finance discussion list.* finance-dl@weg.isu.edu (8 Jan. 1999).

Note that APA style calls for citing nonretrievable sources only in your text (see p. 58). Model 11 shows the format for an archived posting, which is retrievable.

10. A posting to a newsgroup or forum

Cramer, S. (2000, March 26). Recent investment practices. news:biz.investment.current.2700 (3 Apr. 2000).

Note that APA style calls for citing nonretrievable sources only in your text (see p. 58). Model 11 shows the format for an archived posting, which is retrievable.

11. An archived posting

Tourville, M. (1999, January 6). European currency reform. *International finance discussion list.* http://www.weg.isu.edu/finance-dl/46732 (2 June 1999).

12. An encyclopedia

White, G. (1997). Ethnopsychology. In R. Wilson & F. Keil (Eds.), *The MIT encyclopedia of cognitive sciences.* Cambridge, MA: MIT Press. http://mitpress.mit.edu/MITECS/work/whiteg_r.html (26 Mar. 1999).

13. A database

U.S. Department of Health and Human Services. (1993, April). Depression is a treatable illness: A patient's guide. *Health services technology assessment texts* (No. 93-0533). http://text.nlm.nih.gov/ftrs/pick?collect=930533 (26 Sept. 1999).

14. A gopher or FTP site

Provide directions to a specific source in one of two ways: give the unique address of the file, as in the example above; or give the address of the home page, a space, and the path to the file, as in this example:

Goetsch, S. (1995). And what about costume? *Didaskalia: Ancient Theatre Today, 2*(2). gopher://gopher.warwicku.ac.uk Didaskalia/Didaskalia: Ancient Theatre Today/1995/03Features/Goetsch (26 May 1999).

15. A telnet site

Johnson, E. (1999, August 7). My house: Come in. *Houses of cyberspace.* telnet://edwin.ohms.bookso.com.7777 @go #50827, press 10 (11 Aug. 1999).

16. A synchronous communication

Wendy_Librarian_. Online integrity (#421). *Internet Public Library MOO.* telnet://moo.ipl.org.8888 @go #421 (4 Jan. 1999).

17. Software

Project scheduler 8000. (1999). Orlando, FL: Scitor.

US Postal Service abbreviations

Alabama	AL	Kentucky	KY	North Dakota	ND
Alaska	AK	Louisiana	LA	Ohio	OH
Arizona	AZ	Maine	ME	Oklahoma	OK
Arkansas	AR	Maryland	MD	Oregon	OR
California	CA	Massachusetts	MA	Pennsylvania	PA
Colorado	CO	Michigan	MI	Puerto Rico	PR
Connecticut	CT	Minnesota	MN	Rhode Island	RI
Delaware	DE	Mississippi	MS	South Carolina	SC
District of Columbia	DC	Missouri	MO	South Dakota	SD
Florida	FL	Montana	MT	Tennessee	TN
Georgia	GA	Nebraska	NE	Texas	TX
Hawaii	HI	Nevada	NV	Utah	UT
Idaho	ID	New Hampshire	NH	Vermont	VT
Illinois	IL	New Jersey	NJ	Virginia	VA
Indiana	IN	New Mexico	NM	Washington	WA
Iowa	IA	New York	NY	West Virginia	WV
Kansas	KS	North Carolina	NC	Wisconsin	WI
				Wyoming	WY